Marketing Propaganda

From attention to the Meaning economy

Francesco Ferzini

To My Family

WHY SHOULD I READ THIS BOOK?

...You may ask your selves.

I would not tell you to read this book. That's your decision. The choice is yours.

Are you interested in understanding how PRopaganda plays on the dynamics of public opinion and how we as humans make sense of and derive meaning from the world around us and use this knowledge to determine where you can focus your Marketing efforts in appealing to your audience to get the desired results?

You might want to know more about the intricacies of the human mind, how it really works and, how we construct our worlds of meaning and, how those meanings affect our experiences and govern our understanding of the world around us and our decision-making processes.

We are passing through a period of (digital-)socialization and marketing has changed. Fundamentally, marketing is a human endeavor. Human attention is scarcer than ever and what really drives people is meaning. What the experiences you provide mean to your audience will largely determine how they will relate back to you.

How is this book structured? My goal was to condense and distill research and knowledge by describing and discussing complex issues in an informal and entertaining tone without erasing their complexity but simply making reading about them, understanding them, and, most importantly, applying them easier to do.

There are no chapters. The wealth of information and ideas is bound up within shorter sections (attention is scarce, remember?). The early parts of the book describe rhetoric and the earliest uses of PRopaganda, moving along on the developments of psychology and neurosciences and how gaining more knowledge about how the mind works and how we create meaning is the key in understanding how people make decisions and attribute meaning to any experience.

As a preliminary remark, before you start reading the book, throughout the text you will find the word "PRopaganda" (capital letters *P* and *R*). This is just a stylistic choice I made for this particular book because to me Public Relations (PR) and Propaganda both have exceptionally similar meanings.

> *"Most people live in a very restricted circle of their potential being. We all have reservoirs of energy and genius to draw upon of which we do not dream."*

(WILLIAM JAMES)

NOT HAVING SPARE TIME

Time has become a scarce commodity in the hectic multitasking globe we live in.

If you do not have some spare time to read the entire book here's a synthetic version of its juice:

> *We live in a complex and interconnected real-time digital world. Some call it the Attention Economy.*

Taking into account the interconnectedness of events, earning attention is vital, but no longer enough.

Success belongs to marketers who have a thorough understanding of individuals' and masses' mental processes and social-connection patterns and how their publics know what they think they know and what their true motives are, and, as a consequence, are able to create and provide them with robust <u>Meaning</u> *to conquer awareness and channel intent toward a desired outcome.*

THE MEANING ECONOMY

Technology developments have been impressive. The web, cybernetics, medicine, artificial intelligence, robotics, nanotechnology, the quest of immortality at Singularity, the quest for transplanting the human brain into robotic units, and human consciousness into the virtual world at Global Future 2045, et cetera.

The new channels of thought and communication have become the greatest medium to reach a potentially universal public, and the approach to information management shifted to treating human cognitive aspects as attention to being a scarce commodity.

Epistemology and semantics have always been core, fundamental traits of human life. The scarcity of consumer attention is no longer a limiting factor when a rich sense of meaningfulness is attributed to any experience. We live in a knowledge-intense semantic world, and we are a semantic and symbolic class of life. Every decision we make is often built around pure emotional states, and we tend to justify our behavior and actions with rational and intellectual thinking. Emotions are governed by meaning and meaning is a man-made creation.

Meaning is the ultimate and most critical element in human life. Just imagine living a meaningless life with no purpose or direction; even in the socialization era, your social sphere and willpower would collapse.

Despite the fact that we live too close to our planet to grasp its wholeness at the outside of our constructed realities, social intercourse between humans still depends on communication, and we need the cooperation of other people for everything we need, want, or desire in our lives. The secret of success lies in effective communication added to compelling and meaningful experiences.

The ability to influence opinions and establish attitudes through PRopaganda is well-known throughout history. The Fathers of PRopaganda developed strategies to mold public opinion, broadcast their word to a large number of people, and manufacture consent. To date, the new media avenues give the opportunity to transmit ideas and relate to and interact directly with others at a tremendous velocity, bypassing the conventional mass media filters, time, and geo-limits.

As a preliminary remark, no two people are alike in the whole world, but established and unified attitudes may be manufactured. The study of meaning—how it is conveyed through language and signs, how it is interpreted, how it affects neurology and the differences that come into play between different cultures—is a basic requirement for every effective communicator.

Blurring the line between virtual and reality, there are a multitude of new highways of thought to approach the public mind. All these means by which human beings communicate to one another, are instruments to propagate opinions and ideas to influence, mold, and form the will of others—in other words, PRopaganda.

Securing attention is the very first step to induce action. But, what's in between before a decision is made? Awareness leads to interpretation, and perceptions are the result of the processing of information governed by the meanings people have created as their worlds of reality. Well-timed and highly relevant content needs to be imbued with meaning. Human nature needs meaning. To seduce minds, it is imperative to get to the heart of things and explore human knowledge and motives, adding meaning to the formula.

How do your publics know what they know and what it means to them?

SYMPOSIUM

The translation of the original Greek word *symposion* literally means "drinking together." In Ancient Greece, the Symposium was a drinking party. Food and wine were served, but heavy drinking was the most enjoyable task. Entertainment was provided as well and could take the form of flute-girls (or boys), singers, games, or performances by hired entertainers. Drinking and kinky entertainment were the norm but by no means the objective of those meetings. The most important aim was debating and creating discourse about a multitude of topics, from philosophy, to emotions, to the difference between genders, and to propose well-educated and argued speeches to the fellow members of the group.

As far as human nature is concerned, Greek philosopher and mathematician Plato was convinced that the study of philosophy was the only way to absolute truth. He did not appreciate any subtle persuasion method, and he was outraged by the Sophists, whom he saw as manipulators.

Sophistry, in fact, means trickery.

At the time, the Sophists were evangelizing the *Dissoi Logoi*, a rhetorical exercise to help people gain a deeper understanding of various topics by suggesting that they look at anything also from the angle of the opponent.

Plato considered their teachings as being clever but misleading argumentations. The Sophists did not believe in any absolute truth and were convinced that everything is debatable because everything is built around human standards. The following maxims are ascribed to a Sophist, Protagoras, and show how they viewed the role of persuasion in society.

"Man is the measure of all things."
"There are two sides of every issue."

Meaning attribution plays a central role in human nature and personality. Being the measure of all things, it creates and governs our realities—a revolutionary view of the philosophical doctrine that the universe is made of something else other than human influence and man-made meanings.

Minds are built around meaning.

RHETORIC NEVER FADES AWAY

Rhetorical skills were highly regarded in Ancient Greece. Aristotle was a Greek philosopher—an expert in a significant number of different subject areas, a polymath. He believed that knowledge is gained only by logic and reason and in using highly vivid imaginary examples tailored to fit and leverage preexisting beliefs in a given context to meet the listener on his landscape. He wrote the first comprehensive theory of influence and persuasion—rhetoric—reconciling the position of his teacher (Plato) and the Sophists. Aristotle found that there are few basic and fundamental skills to deliver convincing and persuasive arguments, the so-called three artistic proofs:

- *Ethos*: the source of the message and the credibility and effectiveness of the communicator;
- *Logos*: the proof, the logic used to support the argument, the substance of the message itself; and
- *Pathos*: the emotional and motivational state of the audience.

Looking forward in time, great Roman orator Marcus Tullius Cicero supported Aristotle's views by arguing that the duties of the orator (what he called the *official oratoris*) are to first establish credibility and then fill the message with sound arguments and the audience with emotions. In his rhetorical handbook for orators, *De Inventione*, Cicero was quoted to say, "*Wisdom without eloquence has been of little help to the states, but eloquence without wisdom has often been a great obstacle and never an advantage.*"

In spite of a few exceptions, such as the fact that the credibility of the communicator might be manufactured and does not depend on the goodwill or character of the author, Aristotle's beliefs are still supported to date by most of the modern social psychology experts. In today's complex world, no one is reinventing the wheel. We communicate to influence and persuade others.

We are still deploying strategies and tactics to ensure that our message is understood, accepted, and acted upon by our audience.

The way we want to.

SPREADING THE WORD

Would you be surprised if I told you that PRopaganda is just a form of communication? It is primarily aimed to influence the attitudes of an audience toward a cause or position; and, fundamentally, it should be a neutral term.

The original Latin word refers to the biological reproduction of flora and fauna. It means to propagate and refers to things that must be disseminated. Nonetheless, the term *PRopaganda* developed a hugely negative connotation by being associated with the World Wars. While to date, the term PRopaganda might evoke images of Swastikas and oceanic crowds of people raising arms to their *Führer*, it is important to note that it was not invented by the Nazis.

The PRopaganda abracadabra as we know it finds its roots in 1622, when the papacy coined the phrase *Propaganda Fide*. Pope Gregory XV, frightened by the spread of Protestantism, founded the *Sacra Congregatio Cristiano Nomini Propaganda* (Sacra Congregatio de Propaganda Fide), which was the missionary arm of the Catholic Church. Later, Pope Urban VIII made it an institution.

The propagation of Faith was a matter of such vital importance for the Roman Curia to demand a great involvement by the whole Ecclesiastical jurisdiction. The Department of the Pontifical Administration had the purpose to coordinate and promote missionary activities, spread Catholicism, and regulate the ecclesiastical affairs in all the non-Catholic countries. It played an important role in the diffusion of Catholicism around the world, especially in Africa, Asia, and the Americas. The Sacred Congregation for the Propagation of Faith is still a Congregation of the Roman Curia for the Evangelization of Peoples (*Congregation pro Gentium Evangelizatione*).

In the classical archives of the University of Notre Dame (*Magnum bullarium Romanum: bullarum, privilegiorum ac diplomatum Romanorum Pontificum amplissima collection)* the translation of the Latin text clearly tells of "*the Will of leading by the springs of the waters of life and place wanders in the pasture of true Faith.*"

In the nineteenth century, as it began with Catholicism, the term PRopaganda was widely associated with the Roman Curia and did not possess any manipulative aura—no negative association with the spread of deceptive lies, half-truths, or false rumors.

Until the First World War.

MANIPULATING PUBLIC OPINION

In history, what we now call *public opinion* has always been molded by leaders, such as monarchs, tribal chiefs, religious figures, princes, and kings. Sovereignty was never open to debate. There were frictions, clashes, fights, and bloody battles to conquer territories, but the opinion of the masses was never taken much into account in order to rule them. It was masters and commanders versus a useless bunch of people.

The Industrial Revolution, a pivotal point in human history, ascended the kings' thrones and led to a major understanding of the importance of public opinion and the need to transmit a positive image to the general populace to gather the support of the broad masses.

The very first marketing steps date back 1786, when the first acknowledged advertising agency ascribed to William Taylor was opened. In 1848, the short publication of the *Manifesto of the Communist Party* was published and, through tireless PRopaganda speeches, became one of the most influential political treatises ever written. In 1894, French social psychologist Gustave Le Bon published his first influential work, *The Psychology of Peoples.* Understanding the increased attention on public opinion and its impact on public policy, politics, and social matters, industrialism introduced new forms of communication and new roles of corporate-to-audience relationships.

Outstanding personalities like Ivy Lee (1877–1934), who is ascribed for having issued the very first press release and often cited in textbooks with reference to the Pennsylvania Railroad issues; two-time Pulitzer Prize winner Walter Lippmann (1889-1974), who served as propagandist for the Great War; and Sigmund Freud's nephew, Edward Louis Bernays (1891–1995) are often mentioned as the most influential people behind the birth of public relations and modern PRopaganda methods.

Bernays combined the teachings of various social psychology experts with the psychoanalytical studies of his uncle, arguing that "*modern propaganda is a consistent, enduring effort to create or shape events to influence the relations of the public to an enterprise, idea or group.*" He is still considered the pioneer of the scientific technique of shaping and manipulating public opinion, which he used to refer to as the "*engineering of consent.*" Along with Walter Lippmann, Bernays was an integral part of the Committee on Public Information (CPI) of the United States during the First World War, aiming to "*Make the World Safe for Democracy.*" He was convinced that "*the conscious and intelligent manipulation of the organized habits and opinions of the masses is an important element in democratic society.*" Bernays' views of democracy meant that a highly educated élite would be responsible for orchestrating the landscape from which the general populace derives opinions to create and crystallize their will and impressions.

Things were changing toward a better understanding of the collective perception.

And how to manipulate it at will.

"All truth passes through three stages. First, it is ridiculed. Second, it is violently opposed. Third, it is accepted as being self-evident."

(ARTHUR SCHOPENHAUER)

WORLD WAR I PROPAGANDA

The 1911 *Encyclopaedia Britannica* online describes PRopaganda as being *"the term applied to a concerted scheme for the promotion of a doctrine or practice; more generally, the effort to influence opinion; by a false analogy from such plural words as 'memoranda,' frequently applied to the means by which a propaganda is conducted. The objective of a propaganda is to promote the interests of those who contrive it, rather than to benefit those to whom it is addressed; in advertisement to sell an article; in publicity to state a case; in politics to forward a policy; in war to bring victory. This differentiates it from the diffusion of useful knowledge; the evangel of a mission; publication of the cure for a disease. In such objectives there may be a secondary advantage to the contriver, but to benefit the subjects of the effort is the leading motive. Similarly those engaged in a propaganda may genuinely believe that success will be an advantage to those whom they address, but the stimulus to their action is their own cause. The differentia of a propaganda is that it is self-seeking, whether the object be worthy or unworthy, intrinsically, or in the minds of its promoters."*

Aggressive tactics and strategies to control opinions have always been used in some way and date back to remote antiquity. A better understanding of mass psychology and the rise of the mass media made it possible to deploy the PRopaganda machinery with insidious intent. Every nation that took part in the World War from 1914 to 1918 used elaborated propagandistic tools for a variety of reasons to justify involvement and as a means to procuring money and men and to provide resources to sustain their military campaigns. By 1915, governments and their intelligence departments selectively deployed a wide range of strategic media tools to mobilize domestic support and to disseminate information outside nations' borders.

George Creel, the director of US Office of War Information, wrote, "*It was the fight for the minds of men and conquer of their convictions. It was in the recognition of public opinion as a major force that the Great War differed from essentially from all previous wars.*" This shows an important shift in human thinking that underlines the growing importance of gaining consent by molding the opinions of the masses that once were not even taken into account by ruling authorities and royal families.

During wartime, PRopaganda was no more about true Faith. Instead, it showed itself as being a powerful means to mold public opinion and attitudes. By peeling off the Christian-Catholic aura but maintaining a religious-like sentiment, PRopaganda exposed its worst and sinister side. The dissemination of atrocious storytelling through literature, pictures, films, and any other possible form of communication was put in place for the purpose of mobilizing hatred against Germany. Captivating and subtle stories were incessantly aimed at humiliating and dehumanizing the enemy.

In his excellent studies, Le Bon tells that, in crowd psychology, convictions are extremely powerful and sympathy may become adoration while, on the other hand, antipathy leads to intolerant and ferocious hatred. All the crowds show similar characteristics. Depending on the nature of the exciting cause influencing them, they may be idealistic and highly suggestible. For this reason, PRopaganda speeches have the tendency to be one-sided and play on simple heuristics by making the counterpart an object of hatred. Actions and behaviors are then to be considered as righteous in the name of moral justifications. Under the magic spell of a strong leader, a nation as a whole might become a killing crowd displaying clear homicidal traits.

Victory is promised.

THE AMERICAN GOSPEL

To Bernays, domination is not a product of armaments, wealth, or policies, but it is based upon the consistency of a compact solid unity opposed to a high degree of disunity. In his masterpiece on *public opinion*, Lippmann cites three distinct ways to obtain cohesive force. The first is amalgamating and stabilizing cohesiveness through reciprocation and favoritism—what he defined "*patronage and pork*"—the second is "*governing by terror and obedience*," and the other is "*government based on such a highly developed system of information, analysis, and self-consciousness that the 'knowledge of national circumstances and reasons of state' is evident to all men.*" As far as the third method is concerned, Lippmann adds some important considerations to George Creel's account of his fight for the minds of men and for the conquest of their convictions by saying that:

"*Mr. Creel had to assemble machinery which included a Division of News that issued, he tells us, more than six thousand releases, had to enlist seventy-five thousand Four Minute Men who delivered at least seven hundred and fifty-five thousand, one hundred and ninety speeches to an aggregate of over three hundred million people. Boy scouts delivered annotated copies of President Wilson's addresses to the householders of America. Fortnightly periodicals were sent to six hundred thousand teachers. Two hundred thousand lantern slides were furnished for illustrated lectures. Fourteen hundred and thirty-eight different designs were turned out for posters, window cards, newspaper advertisements, cartoons, seals and buttons. The chambers of commerce, the churches, fraternal societies, schools, were used as channels of distribution. Yet Mr. Creel's effort, to which I have not begun to do justice, did not include Mr. McAdoo's stupendous organization for the Liberty Loans, Nor Mr. Hoover's far reaching propaganda about food, nor the campaigns of the Red Cross, the Y.M.C.A, Salvation Army, Knights of Columbus, Jewish Welfare Board, not to mention the independent work of patriotic societies, like the League to Enforce Peace, the League of Free Nations Association, the National Security League, nor the activity of the publicity bureaus of the Allies and of the submerged nationalities."*

The Great War had begun almost three years before America entered it. The PRopaganda outreach of the Committee on Public Information effort was massive. A young soldier who was fighting at the German front understood the value of large scale PRopaganda and, when talking about a great and direct forum of listeners, he believed that what's called public opinion is just based on the individual experience and knowledge and that *"most public opinion results from the way public matters are presented to the people through an overwhelmingly impressive system of controlled information."* By far, he was convinced that the most important aspect of PRopaganda and political education was to create frames of mind through the greatest mass-education machine: the press.

In 1921, when Adolf Hitler joined the German Workers' Party, he immediately took charge of all PRopaganda with the aim of distributing the Party's idea to a large audience. He believed that PRopaganda was the means to implant a New World concept doctrine to replace the growing Jewish Marxist ideology in people's heads.

And compel them to accept it.

!HALT THE HUN!

The Hun is a derogatory name.

It was widely used by the Americans and the British to depict the German Army during the first world conflict. The term Hun dates way back in history and was taken from the Chinese Boxer Rebellion. The Allied PRopaganda widely used it to characterize the Germans as vicious and barbarous, suggesting that German soldiers were keen to the most fearful and outrageous behavior and worst kind of conduct ever. All the sources of information were controlled by governments, and infamous stories were spread to ensure the public's compliance and to break the enemy's psychological defenses.

The German Realm leaders were caught off guard and their counter-PRopaganda efforts to make the Allied forces look ridiculous in comic books did have the opposite effect, weakening their soldiers' morale on the battlefield.

Germany was defeated by the Allies and, on the 11 November 1918, the armistice signed by the parties ended the fighting. Later, on 28 June 1919, le *Traité de Versailles* was signed and Germany, along with Hungary and Austria, were forced to accept responsibility for having caused the war.

German pride, prestige, and power were completely demolished.

FROM "MEIN KAMPF" TO "TOTALER KRIEG"

After the First World War, Germany could not recover. It was deep economic recession.

In 1923, inspired by the Italian Fascist Party's leader Benito Mussolini's March on Rome, Adolf Hitler and other

German nationalists of the Kampfbund (*a league of patriotic fighting societies and the National Socialist Party*) tried to seize the power in Munich in what's historically known as the *Beer Hall Putsch*. The attempted revolution failed. Adolf Hitler was imprisoned.

In 1924, while in jail, Hitler devoted himself to writing the *Mein Kampf* to present his ideas in a two-volume book that contained both autobiographical and ideological views about the state of the world. As a soldier who was absolutely disenchanted by the Great War where he fought, Hitler strongly believed that a key factor for Germany's defeat was the application of PRopaganda by the Allies and the absolute failure of the entire German information system. He was confident that PRopaganda was merely another frightening weapon in the hands of an expert. This led him to investigate the use of PRopaganda, to which he even dedicated two entire chapters of his book.

Hitler defined the proper use of PRopaganda as being a true art that only the Christian-Socialist movement used with masterful skill. According to the uncensored Ford translation, he wrote that he learned an infinite amount from the Allied forces' PRopaganda and that "*the success of any advertising, whether in business or politics, depends on perseverance and consistency. The enemy war propaganda was a perfect model because it was restricted to a few points, targeted exclusively at the masses, and continued with tireless perseverance.*" In Hitler's words:

- "*Propaganda's purpose is not scientific training of the individual, not to give details or to act as a course of instruction, but directing the masses' attention to particular facts, occurrences and necessities. The importance of these facts can only be brought in their views by the means of propaganda.*"

- *"The art of propaganda consists in putting a matter so clearly and forcibly before the minds of people that it creates a strong conviction in everyone. It is essential to success that propaganda reinforces the reality of the facts that are promoted, the necessity of what is being promoted and the just or rightness of its character."*

- *"All propaganda must appeal to the common people in tone and in form and must keep its intellectual level to the capacity of the least intelligent person at whom it is directed. In other words, the intellectual level must be lowered as the mass of people it is intended to reach grows. If it is necessary to reach a lot of people, as in the case of national propaganda for the continuation of war, you can never be too careful about controlling the intellectual level of Propaganda."*

- *"The less science is involved, the more emotions are involved. Understanding the emotional patterns of the great masses and using proper psychology to get their attention and touch their hearts is the true art of propaganda."*

- *"The purpose of propaganda is not to be a constant source of interesting diversion for unconcerned smart gentlemen, but to convince the masses! The masses are slow moving, and it may take a long time before they are ready even to notice something. Only constant repetitions of the simplest ideas will finally stick in their minds."*

- *"The more completely propaganda has worked its magic among all the masses and the more the organization which has been built is made exclusive, rigid, firm, the more likely the final triumph of an idea becomes."*

- *"If propaganda is to be effective, it must aim in one direction only."*

- *"I am very proud, even today, that I was able to effectively counter their propaganda and eventually to best its creators at their own work. Within two years, I had become the master in the art of propaganda."*

Mein Kampf volumes were published and soon started to grow in popularity outside National Socialist German Workers' Party (NSDAP) adepts. With Adolf Hitler's ascent to power, the book became tremendously popular, confirming Hitler's thinking that "*every great world-changing movement driven by an idea must first spread his idea using propaganda*" and that "*after propaganda has converted the entire population over to an idea, only a handful of men are needed to finish the job.*" The rule was absolute obedience to leadership. The NSDAP was never meant to be a follower or servant. The objective was to be the master of public opinion and the masses' lord.

A few years later it was *Totaler Krieg.*

Total war and mobilization.

NAZI PROPAGANDA

In *A Chronology and Glossary of Propaganda in the United States,* Richard Alan Nelson defines PRopaganda as "*a systematic form of purposeful persuasion that attempts to influence the emotions, attitudes, opinions, and actions of specified target audiences for ideological, political, or commercial purposes through the controlled transmission of one-sided messages (which may or may not be factual) via mass and direct media channels.*" PRopaganda is often considered to be the spreading of information, ideas, and even rumors for the purpose of helping or injuring others. In this particular case, it was no-rules wartime PRopaganda.

Since 1921, Adolf Hitler was in charge of all the German Workers' Party PRopaganda. In 1933, he became the nation's Reich chancellor and devout follower Dr. Paul Joseph Goebbels, who rose to power along with him became the head of the Reich Ministry of Public Enlightenment and propaganda apparatus, responsible for controlling the press and the culture of the entire German Country. Adolf Hitler's knowledge on PRopaganda began to be systematically executed and transformed into a highly sophisticated machine deploying carefully crafted tactics to persuade, deceive, misrepresent, and subjugate the media and subdue minds and, nonetheless, to attack to the opposition by any reasoned yet cynical means.

Tight control of every approach with the audience was in place to imprint the desired impressions in people's minds. Nevertheless, this was absolutely not a Nazi prerogative. Globally, other war protagonists were working just as hard in using all the available tools to influence their publics.

In Germany, the Nazi Party took complete control of all the media, from the radio to the television and from arts to cinema. All the sources of information were under control. Public opinion was shaped through PRopaganda, the control of the news flow and censorship within (and outside) the country's borders.

The Nazi Party hierarchs believed that the repetition of simple affirmations, slogans, and images were to increase the validity of the message itself and, in the long run, the message would be perceived as true and believable and win the heart of the masses to which the messages were aimed. They propagated messages with a very high and hammering frequency through all the available communication channels.

Everything had a dramatic aura—from symbols to architecture and uniforms and from speeches to selected crowds. Agenda-setting was extremely important. Everything was scrupulously organized with intent.

The use of all the conceivable PRopaganda tools was systematic. Nothing was by chance. In 1943, in front of a large and carefully selected audience at the Sports Palace in Berlin, Goebbels delivered his most famous speech:

*"I ask you: Do you want total war? If necessary, do you
want a war more total and radical than anything that we
can even yet imagine?
Rise up, people, and unleash the storm!"*

With skillful PRopaganda, the battle of a man, an ideology, a book, or a manifesto may even spark a world war.

THE CROWD AND MASS MANIPULATION

Is there a mysterious wizardry or magic formula to manufacture mass moods? Masterpieces on the psychology and behavior of the masses highlight that people behave very differently when in a crowd and that the unconscious mind plays a great role in determining the behavior of what it is considered, as social philosopher Everett Dean Martin highlighted, as being much more than an aggregation of people—a form of psychic behavior, a state of mind by itself.

Effective and persuasive communication has always been used since antiquity in many fields. PRopaganda is considered a consistent, enduring effort to orchestrate circumstances and events to influence relations, attitudes, and perceptions. Its techniques exploit all the systems of communication that permit the exchange of thoughts and ideas, leveraging all the public's information sources and media channels to build opinions.

There is a thin difference between crowd manipulation and PRopaganda. If we use the example of Nazi Germany we easily notice that the dissemination of information and masterful use of PRopaganda was put in place by Goebbels, whereas the leader, or mass manipulator, was to be found in Adolf Hitler. Back to Aristotelian logic, we might infer that

PRopaganda prepares the stage for the crowd manipulator to effectively project and transmit a reinforced message.

As Martin points out on the basis of Lippmann reasoning, "*The average man is a dogmatist. He thinks what he thinks others think he is thinking. He is so used to propaganda that he can hardly think of any matter in other terms.*" The mass is continually exposed to suggestion, and general sentiments are affected by stereotypes, symbolic phrases, and affirmations to gain assent. As many public opinion masters point out, thought is the function of an organism, the mass is not.

The individual human mind is easily influenced and the crowd, taking into account the distinguishing characteristics of groupthink and the great power of public indoctrination, even more.

STAGECRAFT

James Crook said, "*A man who wants to lead the orchestra must turn his back on the crowd.*" Presumably, he was not referring to the general characteristics of crowds as explained by Le Bon:

"*In its ordinary sense the word crowd means gathering of individuals of whatever nationality, profession, or sex, and whatever be the chances that have brought them together. From the psychological point of view the expression crowd assumes quite a different signification. Under certain given circumstances, and only under those circumstances, an agglomeration of men presents new characteristics from those of the individuals composing it. The sentiments and ideas of all the persons in the gathering take one and the same direction, and their conscious personality vanishes. A collective mind is formed, doubtless transitory, but presenting very clearly defined characteristics. The gathering has thus become what, in the absence of a better expression, I will call an organized crowd, or, if the term is considered preferable, a psychological crowd. It forms a single being, and is subjected to the law of the mental unity of crowds."*

Crowds express some constant characteristics such as self-flattery and self-adulation. The crowd makes an all-powerful hero out of the public person, the leader, and transforms the individual into a symbolic and constructed personality of what the crowd itself wishes him to be—a God-like figure. In this particular case, turning your back on the beliefs of the fellow members is not recommended as the best possible course of action.

Wherever a group has sufficiently become a crowd, it develops linkages, connections, and a PRopaganda of its own. Messages are disseminated and spread as a contagious infection. The illusion and suggestion added to the process of pathogenic-like contagion leads to multiplying the number of influenced people. As a consequence, to lead crowds, you need not forget the simple leverage techniques proposed by Aristotle and Cicero: source credibility, the substance of the message itself, and the emotional states of the audience.

The content of the message is clearly very important, but the authority of the source and a well-rounded understanding of the anatomy of the public, added to a careful planning of the context to construct the optimum circumstances for public acceptance, are no less vital matters.

Have you ever seen drama, opera, ballet, or musicals? Their theatricality and performance remind me of poetry. Everything is preplanned in its smallest detail to appeal to the public and originate identification. In theater, stagecraft includes constructing and rigging scenery, such as maquillage, stage management, lighting, sound mixing, and all the other activities to prepare the scenery before the show.

Nothing happens by chance. Artists are well-prepared before performing. Everything is planned in advance to establish a favorable climate for the message (or the show) to be easily accepted and acclaimed.

The context—the stage—the structure and substance of the message, and the knowledge of the public's anatomy strongly influence people's cognitive thinking and responses. Just imagine how perfect an opportunity it was for the Nazis to express to the entire world's assorted mass media their alleged supremacy during the well-planned 1936 Olympic Games held in Berlin.

FASCINATION STREET

Great power is given to ideas propagated by affirmation and repetition, repetition, repetition. Concise and simple affirmations that are repeated over time create beliefs, and, once an opinion is formed, give way to a powerful process of contagion that infects minds and perceptions. Meanings are translated into action.

To grab the power of this influence, you need to understand the general characteristics of the masses. In the complex world we live in and with the aid of the web, it is even simpler than in the past for individuals to acquire the psychological characteristics of a crowd with no visible agglomeration.

Although the group mind is made up of individual minds, it is commonly and widely accepted that the collective mind differs from the isolated person and, depending on the exciting cause and circumstances, the overall psychological intellect diminishes to a primeval level. Gustave Le Bon argued that crowds live in a state of expectant attention which, depending on the circumstances, transforms suggestions and illusions into moral duty and profound convictions.

The mob psychology of crowds expresses the following traits:

- Sentiment of power, egoism, and desire for dominance
- Readiness and willingness to be led by a trusted leader (If a leader is not available, the crowd follows a *mélange* of group clichés and stereotypes.)
- High instinct-like degree of suggestibility and contagion within the group
- Predominance of the unconscious personality and mobility (quickness to act)
- Mob's psychic state is intellectually inferior than the individual's
- Impulsiveness, irritability, intolerance, and dictatorialness
- Credulity and readiness to sacrifice own interests
- Crowds think in images with no logical connection
- Exaggerated morality
- Rudimentary form of reasoning
- Group inertia and laziness
- Tendency to hold and defend beliefs
- Inability or unwillingness to welcome opposite views
- Homogeneity
- Leading figures and victorious actions are transformed into symbolical meanings

As a consequence, the crowd mind is not limited to the ignoramus. The cultured man and the unlearned find themselves being incapable of independent and critical thought when they find themselves in a crowd. Groupthink is made up by impulses, learned habits, and emotional states. Simple image-like ideas and concepts transformed into symbols deceive and subjugate; dramatic and theatrical images stir the imagination and wake up the innate and dormant instincts by hallucinating minds and hearts.

Reasoning is non-existent when faced either with the infatuation of the moment or the unshakable beliefs and prejudices that formed over time. Sentiments and feelings are exaggerated, and any attempt to use logical reasoning would have the same result as speaking tech jargon versus popular lingo.

People are conditioned by the unconscious workings of their minds, and, out of isolation, individuals easily fall under the influence of a leader. As Niccolò Machiavelli once said, *"men are very simple in their minds."* They can easily fall under the spell of a leading figure.

Le Bon's findings demonstrate that crowd behavior might be quite peculiar because of immediate exciting causes or remote factors. It might be that a short term "passing-by" opinion infects minds or ancient beliefs, validated and established over time, inspire a stronger sense of duty to arise. Once beliefs are created, it becomes quite difficult to mold opinions. People tend to defend their creed in a religious fashion. The process of contagion is so infectious to shape behavior as it was to create religious devotion. It creates devoted followers who do not question neither the learned stereotypes nor the authority and prestige of their almighty leader.

The powerful influence of words, images, and symbols is not to be undervalued. Fundamentally, their power lies in the meaning attached to them by people. To this, we might add that the world is more complex than ever in history, and distortion of information is unavoidable. We like to think we are rational creatures of reason, but we often rely on emotions, mental habits, prejudices, biases, and learned meanings to create our mental maps to navigate through the world.

Here lies the great power of systematic and skilled PRopaganda in influencing and directing the attitudes and opinions of the masses.

THE INAPPROPRIATENESS OF NOMENCLATURE

Isn't it inadequate to believe marketing equals advertising, public relations is synonym for media relations, and PRopaganda has a sinister meaning? To avoid misunderstandings, it is categorically imperative to get the semantics, denotation, definitions, terminology, and nomenclature right before anything else—and more than ever in human history.

Just have a look at the following definitions from *Britannica* online:

MASS COMMUNICATION: *The technology of modern mass communication results from the confluence of many types of inventions and discoveries, some of which (the printing press, for instance) actually preceded the Industrial Revolution. Tech ingenuity of the nineteenth and twentieth centuries developed the newer means of mass communication, particularly broadcasting, without which the present near-global diffusion of printed words, pictures, and sounds would have been impossible.*

NEWS AGENCY: *Also called press agency, press association, wire service, or news service. Organization that gathers, writes, and distributes news from around a nation or the world to newspapers, periodicals, radio and television broadcasters, government agencies, and other users. It does not generally publish news itself but supplies news to its subscribers, who, by sharing costs, obtain services they could not otherwise afford. All the mass media depend upon the agencies for the bulk of the news, even including those few that have extensive news-gathering resources by their own.*

EDUCATION: *Discipline that is concerned with methods of teaching and learning in schools or school-like environments as opposed to various non-formal and informal means of socialization (e.g. rural development projects and education through parent-child relationships).*

HISTORY: *Discipline that studies the chronological record of events (as affecting a nation or people), based on a critical examination of source materials and usually presenting an explanation of their causes.*

MARKETING: *Its principal function is to promote and facilitate exchange. Though marketing, individuals and groups obtain what they need and want by exchanging products and services with other parties. Such a process can occur only when there are at least two parties, each of whom has something to offer. In addition, exchange cannot occur unless the parties are able to communicate about and to deliver what they offer.*

PUBLIC RELATIONS: *Byname PR. Aspect of communications involving the relations between an entity subject to or seeking public attention and the various publics that are or may be interested in it.*

ADVERTISEMENT: *Also called Ad. A public announcement— generally print, audio, or video—made to promote a commodity, service, or idea though various media, including billboards, direct mail, print magazines and newspapers, radio, television, and the world wide web.*

PROPAGANDA: *Dissemination of information—facts, arguments, rumors, half-truths, or lies—to influence public opinion. Propaganda is the more or less systematic effort to manipulate other people's beliefs, attitudes, or actions by means of symbols (words, gestures, banners, monuments, music, clothing, insignia, hairstyles, designs on coins and postage stamps, and so forth). Deliberateness and a relatively heavy emphasis on manipulation distinguish Propaganda from casual conversation or the free and easy exchange of ideas.*

INFORMATION PROCESSING: *The acquisition, recording, organization, retrieval, display, and dissemination of information. In recent years, the term has often been applied to computer-based operations specifically. In popular usage, the term information refers to facts and opinions provided and received during the course of daily life: one obtains information directly from other living beings, from the mass media, from electronic data banks, and from all sorts of observable phenomena in the surrounding environment.*

Are there similarities? All the definitions refer to information processing and dissemination of information. Oversimplifying, we obtain information from a multitude of sources offered by our surrounding environments. We process all the information provided and received over our lifetime. We learn and we make up our minds. We grow and develop.

Since early childhood someone has been trying to educate us—our families, the education system, the military, the government, and other organizations and associations. Every time we turn on the TV or the radio there is someone trying to convince us that their product or service is the very best.

You absolutely need it. Buy!

The same happens with a book, a brochure, a magazine, a billboard, an image, or a manifesto. Someone is trying to convince us to think about something in a certain way and to induce action. Marketers, advertisers, counselors, and politicians are working hard to have us buying from them, voting for them, subscribing to their website and to convince us that they have our best interest in mind.

Isn't all of the above some sort of indoctrination through PRopaganda?

THE MASS MEDIA AND THE MASS ECONOMY

The mass media have always been intended as means to communicate to a large audience. Control over the masses through the dissemination of controlled information has always been a major interest of corporate giants and governments to approach and architect public opinion, behaviors, and minds.

Advertisers, for instance, use common PRopaganda features, such as repeated exposure to their messages, to leverage familiarity. They repeat their theme over and over trying to leverage consumers' heuristics extensively to secure agreements and purchases.

Economist Edward S. Herman and linguist Noam Chomsky argue in *Manufacturing Consent: The Political Economy of the Mass Media* that "*the mass media serve as a system for communicating messages and symbols to the general populace. It is their function to amuse, entertain, and inform, and to inculcate individuals with the values, beliefs, and codes of behavior that will integrate them into the constitutional structures of the larger society. In a world of concentrated wealth and major conflicts of class interest, to fulfill this role requires systematic propaganda.*" Further developing and discussing Martin's theory that the crowds are more than a physical aggregation of people, Bernays said that "*readers of advertisements, recipients of letters, the solitary listener at a radio speech, readers of the morning newspaper are all mysteriously part of the crowd-mind.*" To this regard, it is important not to fail to grasp the value of enlisting established points of view and the active role the audience plays. The press, for instance, has always enjoyed great importance in guiding public opinion. Lippmann wrote that "*every newspaper, when it reaches the reader, is the result of a whole series of reflections as to what items shall be printed, in what position they shall be printed, and how much space each shall occupy and what emphasis each shall have."*

The selection of news must fit public pressure, taste, opinion, criteria, and interpretation. These aspects forcefully come into play because, as Bernays argued, *"the very fact that newspapers must sell to the public is evidence that they must please the public and in a measure obey it."*

In *Manufacturing Consent*, Herman and Chomsky, propose a set of filters that make up a PRopaganda model and fit the premises for the public's interpretation of what they refer to as being systematic biases. The size, ownership, and profit orientation of the mass media refers to the limitation on ownership requiring large-size investment for newspapers, and the rise of the TV industrial complex led to a greater integration of the mass media into the market system. The mass media became structurally and mutually dependent with powerful and profit-oriented businesses closely tied with corporations, banks, and governments. The influence on the news choice was inevitable.

The advertising-based system negatively affected the working-class press and even the idea of a free market economy where the end user is to decide on purchases. The mass media are interested in a clustered quality audience with buying power and in keeping their flow levels. More advertising time leads to additional revenue from the price of commercials and, in turn, to the marginalization or erasing *in totum* of programs that might interfere with the main purpose: the dissemination of selling messages and the sustaining of ratings and revenue.

The *"symbiotic relationship with powerful sources of information by economic necessity and reciprocity of interests"* means that, in order to meet news demands and schedules, the media concentrate its resources (e.g. reporters) where the action is. Often, reliable sources of information sweep from governments to corporations due to the fact that they maintain a high status of authoritative credibility; hence, news coming from these sources is presumed to be truthful. As a consequence the costs of accurate research are avoided. In turn, the law of reciprocity comes into play and personal relationships are transformed into a state of privileged and mutual dependency between the parties. Furthermore, the news management is designed to produce flaks (considered as being negative responses to media statements or programs that might take various forms, from individual action to organized boycott) to reinforce the strength of the news management itself. Last but not least, the fifth filter refers to the political control mechanism against the ideology of communism.

The five filters result in narrowing the range of the news passing through the mass media gatekeepers and might become the basis of extensive PRopaganda campaigns attuned to the ruling élite interests. As Herman and Chomsky argue, "*a propaganda approach to media coverage suggests a systematic and highly political dichotomization in news coverage based on serviceability to important domestic power interests. This should be observable in dichotomized choices of story and in the volume and quality of coverage. Such dichotomization in the mass media is massive and systematic: not only are choices for publicity and suppression comprehensible in terms of system advantage, but the modes of handling favored and inconvenient materials (placement, tone, context, fullness of treatment) differ in ways that serve political ends.*" Content is created, filtered, and distributed to manufacture Consent.

This is somewhat backed up by Lippmann thinking, which argues that "*The creation of consent is not a new art. It is a very old one which was supposed to have died out with the appearance of democracy. But it has not. It has, in fact, improved enormously in technique, because it is now based on analysis rather than rules of thumb. And so, as a result of psychological research, coupled with the modern means of communication, the practice of democracy has turned a corner."*

In his famous speech at Berkley (1962), English writer Aldous Huxley said that the environment is changed in order to change the individual. Over time, there have been the political revolutions, economic revolutions, time of reformation, and religious revolutions aimed indirectly at human beings by modifying their surroundings with the (ab)use of all the available devices to standardize population and create produced models of human beings—a whole series of techniques to manufacture consent and enable the controlling oligarchy to get people to love their servitude.

To date, totalitarian control of the sources of information still exists, and a censored democracy of deceiving PRopaganda is more than widespread, even though the new media channels offer new ways to dialogue between human beings.

Isn't this another revolution?

The communication revolution of creating universal consent.

STOP STEALING DREAMS

Seth Godin's manifesto Stop Stealing Dreams (what is school for?) offers a thought-provoking view on what school is for. He argues that the economy has changed while the school has not. School was invented to create a constant stream of compliant factory workers to the growing businesses in the 1990s. This objective is no longer needed.

If you look at the big picture, industrialized societies all live by some standards of uniform and accepted beliefs, values, and social codes of conduct and laws. Most people have been transformed into routine-automatons by indoctrination since childhood. Scholarly research tells that children's creativity is suffocated by the education system. The school curriculum does not teach creativity, leadership skills, or independent thinking. The education system teaches what is in the government's interest by unnecessary heavy loads of inadequate and trivial data to be learned by memory instead of the essential knowledge needed in life.

Not only do schools create compliant factory workers, students' minds are molded by leveraging credulity in their goodwill aiming at discipline and compliance. They create good fellow citizens with no intellectual courage and critical doubt abilities—indoctrination to fit a system that is created *Ad Personam.*

Over the last century, past events have been falsified and history is still providing a falsified message to students who are too ready to believe and do not go the extra mile to do some additional research to find the truth, blindly believing what they are taught. On the same line, present events that are brought to our attention by the mass media follow the same principles. News is manipulated to get compliance. We live in a world inundated by trash TV programs, we buy products and services we do not need, and we have been educated on lies and inoculated by overly advertised artificial values by people attempting to modify our opinions and conduct.

In schools, students passively obtain information; obeying is mandatory and learning by the book is what's needed to move on. Pass-degree knowledge-play acting is (usually) enough.

History is made by those who tell the story. It is subjective as opinions are just someone's opinions. History is the replica of factual knowledge that cannot absolutely mirror the truth of the occurrence without being biased. Facts and events are interpreted, encoded, and wrapped into a moralized aura and re-presented into a stereotyped ecosystem for "*what operates in history is not the systematic idea of a genius who formulated it, but shifting imitations, replicas, counterfeits, analogies and distortions in individual minds,*" as Lippmann said.

Being obedient and diligent are the main requirements when you're at school. Being manageable is a next step of the institutional circle of discipline: the work setting. Initiative, will to investigate, critical judgment, passion, and other qualities, such as leadership and character, are surely not learned sitting at a school desk and are sometimes even despised by autocratic business managers.

The naïve acceptance of these superficial fruits of absolute cerebral submission of creative thought and intellectual superiority is no more desirable in the era we live in and lead to profound indecision and lack of decision-making abilities.

What's needed is not materialistic selfishness but a rich conceptual repertoire of relationships between authentic meanings.

PUBLIC RELATIONS

This art is often misunderstood and equated to media relations, crisis management, or covert operations.

Professor Clarke L. Caywood describes Public Relations (PR) as "*the profitable integration of an organization's new and continuing relationship with stakeholders including customers by managing all communications contacts with the organization that create and protect the brand and reputation of the organization.*" The UK Chartered Institute of Public Relations defines PR as being the discipline that looks after reputation, with the aim of earning understanding and support and influencing opinion and behavior; it is the planned and sustained effort to establish and maintain goodwill and mutual understanding between an organization and its publics.

PR may even be depicted as the field of study of the public mind and its interactions. Since birth, PR techniques became one of the most important weapons in the hands of any business on earth. Conscious and intelligent manipulation of the organized habits and opinions of the collective masses were (and are) masterfully put in place by governments, businesses, cults, religions, and individuals.

The manipulation and dexterous use of images, symbols, and slogans inevitably plays on individual and mob psychology by leveraging emotions, psychic states, heuristics, and social biases. Lippmann wrote about the representations of a man-made environment and feelings aroused by constructed mental imagery. He drew a distinction between the real world and the pictures in people's heads by adding that, if an event is not experienced, the feeling might be aroused by mental images and *"until we know what others think they know, we cannot truly understand their acts."*

For over a century, since the corporate world and governments started to pay due attention to public opinion, facts and ideas have been broadcasted through the mass media to orchestrate public acceptance and consent. Businesses run on huge marketing expenditures, and PR professionals worked behind the scenes to have journalists tell their stories.

Ink, airtime, advertising.

A sound understanding of the anatomy of the audience became vital to any business, and the whole PRopaganda arsenal aimed to channel complex human emotions toward a desired outcome: to tell people what you want them to believe by manipulating information and preparing a stagecraft of beliefs to root your message.

A subjective interpretation of the reality itself that has now become an even greater ongoing effort through all the new media to approach the public is that Public Relations is no longer about press releases, traditional pitching mentality, and hits. As PR expert Todd Defren pointed out, it's frequently distributing relevant and well-timed content via the right channels to boost credibility and findability.

However, PR is not only an online issue. Public Relations is about knowing and understanding the public mind and creating the circumstances to earn attention, consolidate meanings, crystallize opinions, and build goodwill on every occasion, no matter between actions, events, or via any other channels of thought and communication.

Public Relations is the result of all the interactions between all the parties involved.

DISSEMINATING SEEDS

Successful businesses are the ones that create or predict and are ever ready to make the shift and change as the public mind changes to conform to a fundamental public acceptance. Traditional Mass Media are steadily declining and, to date, there are literally hundreds of relatively inexpensive alternatives to reach a potentially universal audience.

The consumers' buying cycle is not the same for everyone, and annoying direct sales pitches to urge to buy "Right Now!" are no more a tempting and desirable game. The product, service, or idea shall become desirable by recommending itself through acceptance, connections, relationships, and word-of-mouth/mouse.

Everything we do matters. Modern techniques must not merely take into account the individual or the mass mind alone *but,* quoting Bernays, *"also and especially the anatomy of society, with its interlocking group formations and loyalties. The individual must not be seen as a single cell in the social organism but as a cell organized into the social unit. Touch a nerve at a sensitive spot and you get an automatic response from certain specific members of the organism.*" The circumstances for modifying the public's interpretation of their subjective realities shall be created by developing awareness, engaging people, and helping them build a connection among themselves to share a meaningful Gospel.

The modern media make it easy and quick to bring ideas to the awareness of a chosen audience. However, the key is not asking people to buy from you. It is to obey the audience by understanding their sentiments and transmit new ideas embodied with meaning through their preferred channels to build healthy, trustworthy, and long-lasting relationships.

Meet your audience on their ground and disseminate your appealing PRopaganda seeds.

Flowers will grow.

THE PLANNING FUNDAMENTALS

To plan a campaign, wrote Bernays, the following four requisites must be met:

- "*Calculation of resources, both human and physical; the manpower, the money, and the time available for the purpose;*
- *As thorough a knowledge of the subject as possible;*
- *Determination of objectives, subject to possible change after research; specifically, what is to be accomplished, with whom and through whom;*
- *Research of the public to learn why and how it acts, both individually and as a group.*"

Any business is the result of all the interactions between the parties involved. Objectives must be related and enlisted to the audience whose consent is to be obtained. The goal is to have the public be absolutely convinced by the soundness of new concepts or ideas. News needs to be imbued with appealing meanings to strike the minds and develop public acceptance to induce to action.

Tools change. The fundamentals do not.

FROM PRINTING PRESS TO INTERNET

According to writer Clay Shirky, in the world's history, there are four periods that qualify for the label "Revolution" in the media-changing landscape.

Printing Press Movable Type: The first known movable type was created in China, during the Song Dynasty, around 1040 AD. It was then Johannes Gutenberg who started the printing revolution by inventing a process for mass producing movable type. He introduced it in Europe around 1439. The establishment of trade links due to newly discovered sea routes by Christopher Columbus and Vasco Da Gama facilitated the global spread of the printing press.

Two-Way Communication: Long distance text messaging via some signaling technology was invented about 200 years ago and found its name in the word *Telegraph*. Soon, a real-time and point-to-point communication system that allowed two people separated by long distances to talk to each other was given birth—the Telephone.

Recording Media (other than Print): It was then the turn to have sounds, music, and pictures all encoded into physical objects. These inventions led to transmitting signals by modulating electromagnetic waves and to telecommunication mediums for transmitting and receiving moving images and sounds.

Radio and Television: Radio and TV started to become commonplace about one hundred years ago. They are still commonplace in our homes as sources of information and entertainment. They are still used by businesses and institutions to vehicle advertising and favor stereotypes plus moral judgments to limit critical thinking and influence the entire social set.

The Internet: The web is the network of networks—a global system of interconnected computer networks that serves billions of users worldwide.

For over a century, the primary medium for spreading influential appeals was found in the Mass Media as they were the primary source of information. As Internet rapidly became a complementary source of information, the naïve acceptance of the fruits of unilateral advertising, sales pitches, obsessive promotional activities and direct marketing activities started to diminish. These practices are now the objects of complaints for many. To date, there are many new highways for companies to deliver their PRopaganda— cost-effective channels to reach a potentially universal (and interested) audience directly.

Some say that the message is much more important than the medium; however, if you cannot control every source of information both might be put on the same level of importance, depending on the recipient. Fundamentally, it is all about PRopaganda and the spreading of intentionally persuasive communication, information, and ideas and having your audience at the very center of all your efforts.

The effectiveness of a persuasive message starts from a thorough knowledge of the anatomy and preferences of the recipients, especially on how they interpret information, and what you, your company, and the experience you provide means to them and conditions how they relate to you.

Globally, the web revolutionized almost everything.

Not the human mind.

MEDIA CONTROL

In the evolving scheme of things, the rapid rise of the web forcefully changed how the news is produced and diffused. The Internet is now a critical source of diverse news. Information is available 24/7. News stories are fragmented and decentralized. Readers have the opportunity to find whatever information they are looking for from many sources, make up their minds, and even publish their point of view with regard to anything without being filtered by news agencies and monopolies.

As human beings, we have the tendency to minimize thinking efforts, and we do heavily rely on heuristics (shortcuts) to make sense of, and not feel overwhelmed by, the tons of daily data we process. We do not particularly like to think. Thinking requires energy and we are a lazy species. The media influence over the general public has always been very powerful because people heavily rely on these mediums for their information, *often without questioning the accuracy of a source they regard as being credible.*

Indoctrination through these mediums is not a mystery. Much of the news flow was, and is, provided by the skillful

PRopaganda experts on the government's paycheck to standardize existing points of view and beliefs. In the same way, organizations push out their unilateral propagandistic advertising campaigns to persuade all of us to buy their products or services and create goodwill.

There is a standardized and stereotyped consumerist code of conduct.

INTERNET CENSORSHIP

Irish Nobel prize in literature George Bernard Shaw said, "Assassination is the extreme form of censorship." Internet repression is widely conducted in the People's Republic of China. In North Korea, there is a very limited broadband network, and the country is isolated from the rest of the globe. In Cuba, the web is under surveillance and characterized by censorship. Few other countries are included as well in the "Enemies of the Internet" list by the Reporters Without Borders. Internet censorship exists and instruments, such as content-control software, are widely in use.

New legislation blueprints are said to be solutions to online piracy and copyright infringements, but, having a closer look to the proposed acts, many understand that this is either an attempt to regulate the new media or, more likely, to regain control over the mediums for reaching the masses with the objective of going back in time and keep sailing in the safe (and profitable) waters of the elaborated media landscape of the past. The wave of the future and free communication systems seem to be scary for some and disruptive of the conceptualization of a democratic society as firmly believed by Bernays.

Noam Chomsky argues that there are two different conceptions of democracy: "*One in which the public has the means to participate in some meaningful way in the management of their own affairs and the means of information are open and free,"* or *"A democratic society where the public must be barred from managing their own affairs and the means of information must be kept narrowly and rigidly controlled."*

By saying that there are two visions of democracy—one that presupposes a self-sufficient individual and the other which presupposes an overall regulating everything—Lippmann argues that PRopaganda exists because of some sort of censorship or limited access to what he calls the *"real environment;"* otherwise, it would be impossible to create illusions and disseminate pre-crafted images and facts and information. He says that limiting barriers to knowledge could space from low income, inertia, lack of curiosity toward the human scene or else. As he writes, limitations of access to facts *"are artificial censorships, the limitation of social contact, the comparatively meager time available in each day for paying attention to public affairs, the distortion arising because events have to be compressed into very short messages, the difficulty in making a small vocabulary express a complicated world, and finally the fear of facing those facts which would seem to threaten the established routine of men's lives."*

Ronald Steel, who wrote the foreword to Lippmann's book, is on the same line of thought by saying that the world is too complex to grasp for the average person due to the inability to make sense of the real world as it is. Distortion of information is inescapable and *"the only meaningful public is composed of those people directly interested in an issue. This public has made the effort to learn the facts and weigh the alternatives. But the wider, uninformed public is, and must be limited in its powers."* Contrary to what Lippman claims, to Bernays, PRopaganda is not dependent upon censorship. He considered the precise reverse to be true as PRopaganda being *"a purposeful, directed effort to overcome the censorship of the group mind and herd reaction."*

Often, freedom of choice is just a perception.

COPING WITH CHANGE

With the web, the world became more interconnected, complex, and interdependent than ever before in human history. Rapid technology advancements started a revolution in the way we connect and communicate. Globalization created a forceful alteration of socioeconomic variables and led us in this period of change and uncertainty.

As consumers we could have our voices back after traditional mass media supremacy. Top speed word-of-mouth regained its lost importance. A century of dust was wiped off. We started to connect to the Internet and voice our praise or disappointment about pretty much everything, including products, services, and companies.

In the meantime, we got overwhelmed and tired by thousands of unilateral and unsolicited promo messages. We primarily refer to the web either for buying products and services, to gather information, or even for entertainment. We are happy to browse through search engines, blogs, and social networks either for business or private purposes. We are sick of receiving cold calls. We are tired of the fact that it takes four hours to see a one-hour movie on television because of prime time advertising and we switch to digital TV. We say "no thank you" to receiving tons of direct mail by post. We consider all of this as being time-consuming, unnecessary, and unrequested spam.

We do our best to filter this out and, as a consequence, the traditional ways to do PRopaganda are no longer effective or useful to brands. To date, there are absolutely no guarantees that traditional overplanned clichés could win the real-time business battle in striking the public's mind.

Wasting people's attention is totally counterproductive.

RETURN TO SENDER

Approved by the American Marketing Association Board of Directors in 2007, marketing is defined as being the activity, set of institutions, and processes for creating, communicating, delivering, and exchanging offerings that have value for customers, clients, partners, and society at large.

Since the 1950s firms shifted from producing as much as possible to be more focused on the quality of their products. Selling was the only cause of concern. Then there was a shift from production orientation to focusing on the market. Competition forced the companies to focus on the needs and wants of customers to supply the market on the basis of the demand, not the offer. Companies started to work hard on exercising their audience with hammering advertising full of sexual passion and fighting images (which outranked any other stimuli by appeal) and overpromoting their offers. In the 1990s, other models were proposed, such as the Four Cs, replacing the Ps with Consumer, Cost, Communication, and Convenience; however, the near point did not change much.

In the Information era, many companies and education providers are still concentrated on the *PUSHY Ps of* the marketing mix, a combination of marketing activities that the firm engages in to meet the needs of the targeted market.

- PRODUCT (tangible good or an intangible service),
- PRICE (the amount a customer pays for the product),
- PLACE (the best way to make the product accessible to the consumer),
- PROMOTION (all of the communications used in the marketplace. It includes other disciplines, such as advertising, personal selling, sales promotion, and public relations),

- PEOPLE (the recruitment and useful employment of resources),
- PROCESS (the systems),
- PHYSICAL EVIDENCE (the environment where the service is delivered).

Most organizations are hierarchically built based on military-style operations and strategies. (Almost everything comes from the military; the development of communications devices over the course of human history is a clear example of this.) It is not surprising that many Marketing textbooks refer to military talk when offering tactics and teachings to beat competition. Many business managers even refer to the ancient Chinese book on military strategy ascribed to Sun Tzu, who argued that all warfare is based on deception.

Sun Tzu considered part of the business of a General as creating changes and manipulating them to his advantage. He also put forward the interesting theory of adaptability by saying, "*Just as water adapts itself to the conformation of the ground, so in war one must be flexible.*" Traditional communication channels brought companies to produce goods and services and spread their offerings to the masses. Businesses were used to run on huge marketing and communication expenses, and the average consumer was bombarded by tons of unilateral and unsolicited advertising and promotional activities.

Nowadays, many would like to return unsolicited messages to the sender, as in the famous 1962 song performed by The King, Elvis. Talking back is not only permitted but even encouraged to enchant and engage customers and prospects. The ways of doing business changed and developed over the years as economic variables did.

The rapid development of the Internet revolutionized the world. The principle of understanding the dynamics of public opinion, having a thorough comprehension of the highways along which ideas and opinions travel to reach the public, and creating meaningful value to exceed expectations is more important than ever in history.

DO YOU HAVE MY PERMISSION?

The Industrial Revolution led to mass media supremacy. It started with a means of widely distributing PRopaganda through newspapers and pamphlets. The rise of the printing press coincided with the rise of mass media marketing [Mass market magazines around 1880s, then the radio and TV (respectively 1930 and 1950), Direct Marketing and Telemarketing in the 1980s, and then the web in 1991].

Since the '90s, Internet soon became the carriage of all those media channels, and everyone could access the web 24/7 and even publish content, making use of the new high-speed highways of communication and information.

The idea beyond Seth Godin's Permission Marketing is to obtain interested audiences' permission instead of interrupting people's activities with unrequested advertising and unsolicited promotional messages. This approach takes into account the fact that, in the Information Era, traditional advertising methods are proven not to be as effective as they were in the past.

The fundamental idea is clear: "*Marketers have no longer power over consumers' attention, so stop marketing at people, show them the respect they deserve and let your customers do the marketing for you.*" As Godin argues, for over a century, successful organizations have been built with expensive investments around the traditional TV industrial complex. The explosion of the new media alternatives ended the effectiveness of the traditional leverage techniques. As a result, organizations need to be reinvented because mixing up two, if taken by themselves, fantastic ingredients (new and traditional marketing) will result in a disgusting and ineffective cooking recipe.

A Meatball Sundae.

THE RISE OF INBOUND MARKETING

Permission marketing differs from inbound marketing. The first is a technique that focuses on building a credibility asset and obtaining permission to contact people, while the latter refers to getting found by customers in search engines. To quote marketing strategist and popular speaker David Meerman Scott: "*Before the web came along the only ways to grab attention were to buy expensive advertising, beg the mainstream media to tell your story, or hire a huge sales staff to bug people.*" Everything changed; everyone can now publish their way using the multitude of tools available.

As part of the Social Media series launched by Scott in 2010, Brian Halligan, cofounder and CEO of Internet software company Hubspot, published an entire book, coauthored with Dharmesh Shah, on getting found using Google, social media, and blogs. The web changed the rules of the game. Consumer behavior changed and everyone now turns to the Internet for their needs, wants, and desires. Traditional leveraging techniques are no longer appealing in terms of cost/efficiency and have conquered the bad reputation of being annoying. A pejorative term referred to promoting a product through continued advertising has led to new nomenclature: interruption marketing.

Getting found, generating traffic to one's website, and engaging and connecting people are key aspects of today's business. The basic formula of the sales funnel is to get easily found online, transform visitors into qualified leads and into customers, analyze, and optimize. This means that you need to be familiar with all the new tools available to approach the public mind to earn attention and create high-quality and highly relevant content for your interested audience that will earn their attention. You need to tell stories worth sharing. Educate, inform, and help people solve their problems by exactly matching people's needs, wants, and desires with your service or solution. In other words, make your business meaningful to them.

To manufacture public thought and strike minds, the very first step is to perfectly know the anatomy of your audience and their meaning-making strategies.

"One must understand not only his own business—the manufacture of a particular product—but also the structure, the personality, the prejudices, of a potentially universal public."

(EDWARD BERNAYS)

THE SEMANTIC WEB

Sir Tim Berners-Lee is one of the most outstanding figures behind the web technology developments over the last twenty years. In 1980, while working as an independent contractor at CERN, he built and proposed a project based on a simple hypertext program with the primary objective to store and retrieve information about the structure of a system. The prototype, a method of documenting systems was known as the ENQUIRE system. Despite being considered as the predecessor of the World Wide Web (W3), this system failed.

In 1989 another proposal on Information Management was made. Belgian computer scientist Robert Cailliau collaborated with Tim Berners-Lee in successfully implementing a new communication protocol. Hypertext and a global network (the Internet) were combined. In 1990 the first web server went online and the first web browser was released.

By the end of 1991, the web was publicly available. The net is considered as being a system of interconnected computer networks—*the network of networks*. Over the years, the use of this communication system grew exponentially, and online service platforms made it possible for everyone to create and publish content.

The current web might be considered a global file system—a giant database including a massive amount of information created by a multitude of sources. The main issue lies in the fact that this kind of information is designed for human beings, and machines do not have the capability to understand data as we do. In order to optimize speed and performance in finding documents for any search query, several attempts were made in the past. The first ones were to index data found in the web and then examine content by keyword matching. However, this system is not to be taken for granted. Spelling mistakes, inaccuracies, and the ambiguity of our language make this goal fairly impossible.

With regard to Search Engine Optimization (SEO), Google took further steps by examining links and being able to rank highly connected search results. In any case, until now, it still works because the machines just understand the syntax, not meanings.

Not the semantics.

SEMANTIC TECHNOLOGY

The idea of the Semantic Web is not new. The concept finds its origins in 2001. An article published by *Scientific American* defined it as a new form of web content that is meaningful to computers and that will unleash a revolution of new possibilities. According to the World Wide Web (W3) Consortium, the ultimate goal of the web of data is to enable computers to do more useful work and to develop systems that can support trusted interactions over the network.

The W3 Paradox

Daily, we take advantage of the World Wide Web technology, either for private or business purposes. With computers, we publish, share, read, and search through tons of information. Machines are a central facet to our daily routines; however, they cannot even make sense of the massive amount of information they process.

The underlying principle of the Semantic Web is fairly simple. It involves facilitating the machines to read, understand, and interpret the meaning of information on the web. It is semantics, *the study of meaning*, applied to machines, giving them the opportunity to understand the details of the meaning of relationships, not just connecting pages with the use of links and word matching.

Artificial intelligence is rapidly evolving along with the Internet Revolution's extension. Objects will make themselves recognizable and will possess intelligence on their own. They will have complete access to the interconnected global information network. With the Internet of Things, smart objects will be able to uniquely identify other objects (things) and will be able to talk to each other. Networked devices that recognize the situational context are to be integrated into the environment and to be tailored exactly for our needs.

The human-computer interaction will change.

Forever.

THE WEB NOW

We publish. We share. We read. We search. We like. We process tons of content. Daily.

As an extension of the current technology, there will be a shift from the current web of unstructured information to a knowledge-based framework. Semantic Web Technologies shall enable people to create data stores on the web and writing rules in order to better handle data and build vocabularies. Linked data is empowered by semantic technologies such as RDF, Sparql, OWL, and SKOS. This shall provide a way to express the relationships between pages by allowing machines to understand the semantics of hyperlinked information.

Basically, it is a source to retrieve and access information from the web. Semantic Web Technologies are particularly suitable for combining data sources and for information reuse and might be applied to pretty much everything with regard to information management. For instance, as far as its business uses are concerned, it might be said that the practicality and efficiency of these technologies is to be easily applied from knowledge management to health care or from B2B/B2C services to human resource management plus a wide range of other industries.

The Current Situation

With the current web, there are several barriers to performing daily routines, where collaboration and integrated communication is required because of the following:

- Unstructured data
- Heterogeneous and disparate information
- Several "non-related" sources of information
- Brokering between different content providers
- No personalized matchings

With Semantic Tech

We will enjoy an increase in value with the possibility of working in a much more efficient, effective, and productive way:

- Data integration (combining, organizing, integrating knowledge)
- More personalized offerings = added value to customers
- Better matching by relevance between offer/demand
- Better exploiting implicit content and knowledge
- Combination of services and information from various sources
- Fewer inaccuracies and ambiguities
- Less costs

The Semantic Web Stack, also known as the Layer Cake, illustrates the hierarchy of languages that make up the architecture of the Semantic Web. It is a metadata data-based infrastructure where each layer exploits and uses the capabilities of the below-grounded layers, with the goal of reasoning on the web, within machine processes and global web standards.

The idea of the Semantic Web is thrilling, but there are still more than few challenges to face. The challenges go from the availability of content to the overload of information and from the validity of the Layer Cake to multilingual issues and complete standardization.

To draw an inference from the Semantic Web architecture, our minds are made up of layers of thought that all operate on different levels. The interrelation of all the facets influencing our meaning-making abilities is potentially endless.

CUSTOMIZATION AND MEANING

The web is leading to the increasingly massive use of technology to personalize services and offerings. There is a great emphasis on technology but, at the same time, not enough on how people behave, reason, and make sense of things. Many are so dominated by technology that they sometimes forget that behind a computer or behind a mobile phone there is still a real person. Paradoxically, the study of meaning is applied to machines but has not yet grown in its importance with regard to human beings.

In the near future, services will be more personalized through the endless communication channels. This gives the great opportunity to communicate directly with your audience plus build relationships and communities. Content will be even more powerful than it is at present. Knowing people, decision processes, and how the human mind works is imperative.

The new channels of thought are just new channels to reach the audience as the traditional media were. The only difference is that mass media were used to spreading unilateral messages to the large populace; now, targeted messages can easily travel at a high speed to either individuals or masses, bypassing the traditional filters in a two-way ongoing dialogue.

While it is important to understand how your publics use the new channels of thought and communication, to enchant and seduce minds you must know what their true motives are and what's beyond their drives to build a sound strategy to offer a sublime service to your audience.

The key is what your publics hold in mind and what the experience means to them. Whatever the event, the experience, or the content you share means to them largely determines how they will relate back to you.

ATTENTION PLEASE

Boracay is a little island located off the northwest corner of Panay Island, approximately 315 miles south of Manila. The island belongs to the Western Visayas, one of the three principal geographical divisions of the Philippines. The dog-bone-shaped island is approximately seven kilometers long, with its narrowest spot being less than one kilometer wide.

Boracay's primary tourism beaches are found on the opposite sides of its central area: the main one is White Beach and it is about four miles long. Here you can find resorts, bars, lodges, hotels ranging from five-star to budget accommodation, restaurants, diving centers, and lots of other tourism-related businesses.

The second-most popular beach on the island is Bulabong, famous for water sports, such as windsurfing and kiteboarding. Over the years, Boracay received several awards and its beaches were listed second in the Top Twenty-Five Beaches of the World contest.

If you are not a golf addict, then, apart from an eighteen-hole par seventy-two course designed by professional Aussie golfer Graham V. Marsh, the leisure activities on the island are strictly related to water sports (scuba diving, snorkeling, windsurfing, cliff diving, kiteboarding, and jet skiing). The scenery is captivating and paradisiac. You can relax on the beach and enjoy the sunset, or you can go for a boat trip around the island, snorkel, dive, or just enjoy the breathtaking panorama.

Many young Filipino guys make a living out of leisure activities and they want your attention: *"Hey sir, boat ride around the island? Jet Ski? Parasailing? Banana boat?"*

Too many are eager for your attention. Everywhere you go, the concept of attention economy is mistreated. What did these exaggerated attention-grabbing experiences mean to me?

I was annoyed.

THE QUEST FOR ATTENTION

If you do not get attention, you will not be noticed. If you do not hold attention, you will not be able to persuade. If you do not keep leveraging and managing attention, you will not be able to nurture quality leads. If you waste people's attention, you will not have another chance. Attention has become a scarce commodity as is time. There is no time for complex planning. Things are faster than ever. It's a real-time world.

Attention by itself is not enough; it just means representing something in our minds. It is the higher level of intention that directs people to desired outcomes. As a result, the quest should be on mastering your public's intention for their path to be oriented toward a particular decision or direction and induce action.

Without a robust sense of meaningfulness, there will be no intention.

KISS

Gene "The Demon" Simmons, bassist and vocalist of KISS, said, "Rock is about grabbing people's attention." No one can say that KISS was not able to do that. In today's business world, many focus on buying or earning attention.

Life is an extraordinary network of relationships and connections where effective communication plays an inescapable role. Everything we want or desire involves the cooperation of people. Results don't come from attention only. It might be that something comes into our awareness, but what went in through our eyeballs never re-presents itself into our brain. As such, no meaning is conveyed to the higher levels of our mind and no intention flourishes toward a desired outcome.

TO SCREAM FOR ATTENTION

...is not a good idea. We live in a world where change is the norm, time is subjective, and neither change nor time can be stopped. The clock ticks and changes happen all the time by the ticking of the clock.

Attention is easy to grab. You might walk down the street and start yelling at people. Hey, that is a way to grab other people's attention. However, you do not want that kind of attention. The knowledge-intense Information era differs from the vegetable market square.

Shouting around is no longer a desirable course of action to catch, challenge, and leverage intention. To promote quality meanings as a core value and provide people with a strong enough why is.

TURBULENT TIMES

Industrial revolutions are considered pivot points in human history. These major turning points have affected and influenced everyone in some way. Technological and economic progress gained momentum, and sustained growth was welcomed to the process. Capitalism was critiqued by socialism; Marxism philosophy was born; and intellectual and artistic movements, known as romanticism, supported the hostilities toward the Industrial Revolution. It then grew worse. Now, we find ourselves in turbulent times. Again.

Many countries face huge economic debts, stock markets are shaky, and unemployment rates implacably get higher and higher. The masses find themselves afraid of an uncertain future. The Occupy movement is considered a major public response after thirty years of class war. In the meantime, the web has revolutionized the way human beings communicate among themselves, and industrialized manufacturing-based economies have undergone a transition from the provision of products and services to a new structure based on the provision of services, finances, technology, and data—the e-market of ideas.

Sustained growth is not included in the formula for businesses that do not understand the need to revolutionize their own organizational structure to meet their potential audiences and publics on their ground.

New leaders are needed.

A NEW NORMALITY

New marketing is more than social media tools, Semantic Web, or the Internet of Things. It requires a brand new mindset. We live in a volatile new normality, and new strategic behaviors are needed. The new media are able to reach virtually every kind of audience. On the other hand, lots of companies are still struggling to stick with the status quo and the false belief that what worked in the past will work in the future. They are not open-minded and are not exploiting any opportunity of strategically integrating new ways of doing business in their marketing and communications efforts.

We all know that change is fount of fear, and many people would prefer to safely navigate in the old peaceful waters of the past. This means being on a boat ride to nowhere. Paradoxically, some boat lieutenant commanders are so eager to make profits that they often forget that business is fundamentally about what people perceive at a cognitive level. In a holistic view of the business world, we might infer that the bottom line is people and what's meaningful to them, not money.

The rapid proliferation of the new channels of thought shall lead to an evolutionary fusion between human knowledge and the *cyber-world* to create new meanings that make life easier and simpler.

Smooth.

THE STRATEGIST

Strategy became a popular buzzword in the '60s. Although there are many interpretations and definitions, a business strategy is a fundamental pattern of present and planned objectives, resource deployments, clarity of direction, and necessary flexibility to exploit opportunities with consistency through a thorough understanding of the game, interacting with either the internal and external environment of the organization. The strategist possesses the ability to recognize and exploit opportunities by the clever use of all his weaponry. Flexibility is key.

Information plays a categorically imperative role to all strategies. Communication is never pointless waffle. Effective communication is used to persuade others. The exchange of goods, services, and ideas requires influencing other people. As in game theory (*method of studying strategic decision-making through mathematic models*), you need a plan of action. You need to choose from the options you have, as a player.

The main problem we face with strategy is that we are unique beings, and we all have unique personalities. No two circumstances can be considered alike. Sometimes we fail to recognize reality because we are too used to deceptive PRopaganda, which generalizes and distorts events to recreate a unique perception of the world in our minds. We persuade and influence with words, expertise, trustworthiness, credibility, and even attractiveness and body language.

We prepare the stage with effective communication and dynamic PRopaganda.

We enchant with semantic influence.

STRATEGIC MARKET INTEL

The concept of strategy finds its origins in ancient times. *The Art of War* was *written more than 2000 years ago* and it is still considered a masterpiece, widely read in the academic and business world.

Today, the world is constantly changing, and the business arena is fiercely competitive. In the meaning economy, *information intelligence* is still vital, but *careful planning* is traded with proactive quickness and agility.

Lots of marketing textbooks define strategy on the basis of warfare—a fundamental pattern of present and planned objectives, resource deployments, and the interaction of the organization with its stakeholders and the market (*or the environment*).

All warfare is based on operational military wisdom and deception. In this modern age, the companies that follow these principles by the book will miserably fail. Constant vigilance on information intelligence is vital, but military campaigns are to be left to military troops.

A MESSAGE-DENSE ENVIRONMENT

Technology has developed at a tremendous speed; ideas spread faster than ever in history and may be transmitted to any distance and to any place with no geographical limitation in space and time. News is fragmented and brought to awareness from multiple sources. This may result in being confusing and not conducive to intelligent processing of content or substance. We are practically inundated by content.

Scarcity of information is almost nonexistent. Infobesity reigns but shall not overwhelm authentic meanings by distracting awareness and deflecting attention.

Always seek inner meanings without being distracted by the outer shape of things.

AREN'T YOU DISTRACTED BY INFOBESITY?

You are time-pressured and overloaded by a message-dense world. You are required to be multitasking. Sometimes you find it quite difficult to focus, and you do not find the time or will to understand or find out more about certain topics as you'd wish. You are distracted.

As human beings, we have limited capacity for making sense of the complex world we live in. Distraction leads to confusion, and it is not conducive to clever processing of content. Too many distractions eliminate the substance of the message. We tend to simplify things by relying on heuristics and biases to make decisions. We often do not find the time to investigate any alternative courses of action.

That is the main reason for which your PRopaganda shall be tailored to your specific audience and loaded with semantically emotional content. Messages do not need to be long. On the contrary, short messages work much better in a real-time, message-dense environment. If you must compete for attention, you'd better leverage the basic human need for entertainment and embed your short messages into entertaining content.

No one likes boring people. No one likes boring news. Be clear and entertaining. Deliver short-style PRopaganda content. Evoke pictures and feelings in your audience's head.

Color minds by promoting positive meanings about your desired course of action.

FEMEN

The Mass Media machine to broadcast content is declining. The one-sided relationship with the public and circulation of news as a means to an end is no longer the most effective way to reach the public mind and divulge ideas to build opinions. The brevity of attention and the fact that no one is bonded to loyalty for any conventional media gives to anyone through the web the great possibility to smoothly spread PRopaganda and dialogue at a tremendous velocity through a multitude of channels to a potentially universal audience to earn attention, make connections, and be trusted.

FEMEN was founded by Anna Hustol in 2008. The founder set up the group because she realized that there was a lack of women activists in a Ukraine male-oriented society. According to FEMEN's Google Plus profile, here's their mission and vision:

Our God is woman, our mission is protest, our weapons are bare breasts! *FEMEN (Ukrainian:Фемен) is a Ukrainian protest group based in Kiev, founded in 2008. The organization became internationally known for organizing topless protests against sex tourists, international marriage agencies, sexism and other social, national and international ills. Some of the goals of the organization are: 'To develop leadership, intellectual and moral qualities of the young women in Ukraine' and 'To build up the image of Ukraine, the country with great opportunities for women.' As of late April 2010 the organization is contemplating becoming a political party to run for seats in the next Ukrainian parliamentary election.*

Their PETA-like topless protests get attention. Provocative slogans and nudity as protest have already been used in the past century to grab public attention. It is a way to be heard, and exposure of women's breasts is not considered a criminal behavior around Europe (NB: *In some US states it is*). These girls are a perfect example of modern PRopaganda (a consistent, enduring effort to create or shape events to influence the relations of the public to an enterprise, idea, or group). The context varies (it might be the WEF Forum, FIFA 2012, or else). Stagecraft is in place and their messages are brought to the world's awareness by topless protesters. Highly vivid images and short, simplistic messages are more effective than any thoughtful discussion.

Clearly, it depends on how well-informed the target audience is, and any initial opinions and/or prejudices on the subject at stake still matter a lot. On the other hand, FEMEN activists brilliantly exploit the new media and are able to earn traditional mass media coverage in all their rallies.

They are persistent, cool, and intelligently spread their word with dramatization, vivid terms, and compelling images. They catch the attention, they keep it easily, and motivate to share.

They make their point.

THE SPHYINX OF TRADITION AND CULTURE

Every culture is different. We all have different traditions, rituals, beliefs, laws, food, and yes, even fables. We live in different mental worlds. We are immersed in our private lives and we try to reproduce our abstract conception of the whole world on the simple basis of our experiences.

Take two minutes to see if you are able to spot the following fifteen countries with the help of two clues:

- Hahoe masks and Kimchi
- Cuckoo Clocks and Cheese
- Far West and Burgers
- IceHockey and Peameal Bacon
- Didgeridoo and Vegemite
- Temples and Tom Yam Kung
- Fashion and Pizza
- Volcanism and Smoked Lamb
- Aurora Borealis and Salmon Soup
- Samurai and Sashimi
- Eight World Heritage Sites and Rainbow Cuisine
- Samba and Feijoada
- Systema and Solyanka
- Kung Fu and Meat-Based Geng
- Yoga and Spicy Fish from Kerala

Results:

{Countries: South Korea, Switzerland, USA, Canada, Australia, Thailand, Italy, Iceland, Finland, Japan, South Africa, Brazil, Russia, China, India}.

This was just to show you that our minds live on imagination and thrive on meanings and associations. Furthermore, it underlines the fact that we are all different, we like different things, we come from different cultures, and we are curious. We each see the world under a different light. If we do not understand something, we start to search within our minds what is the significance, the meaning, the semantics of that something. We start what's called transderivational search. We search any possible match, any possible meaning, to make sense of things. It becomes hard if we do not possess the adequate knowledge.

For instance, if I was to ask you to tell me what the following means and, unless you knew Japanese, you would not succeed:

ものいはず
客と亭主と
白菊と

It is a Haiku by Ryota that might be translated in English as:
Without a word,
The guest, the host,
White Chrysanthemums.
Everything in the globe follows the same exact process.
To make sense of the world, we need to know what things do mean.

WE ARE STORYTELLERS

The world is how we expect it to be. It is a stereotyped reality we constructed by inventing meanings. We mold reality and create stories that affect our minds by reproducing the external environment and distorting reality as it better fits our thinking.

Some love discovering and investigating information from the past and history, while others construct future events by speculative manners—a postulated history in a fictional future. One thing is for sure, we like stories. We all love stories starting with "Once upon a time (…)" and ending "(…) and they lived happily ever after," don't we?

To *tell* is the Latin form of "narrate." It means to recount. Storytelling is the conveying of a story using anything, from words to images and sounds. We all are storytellers, aren't we? Each and every day, we all recount our stories. Well-crafted stories persuade.

Well-crafted stories are delivered with intention and purpose. They generate emotions and meet listeners on their playground by influencing their mind. If you are able to create compelling content around something, you have higher probabilities to succeed in focusing and channeling your audience's attention, interest, and intent.

To engage and persuade people, do not focus on too much information; it might be confusing. Instead, nail down a set of topics and develop thought leadership around your area of expertise by recounting your story. People will turn to you for information and advice. Remember to carefully evaluate how well-informed your audience is. Experts will look for details. Non-experts are more likely to look for the big picture.

To stir minds, stories must have a clear purpose. The clear intent of any story is to influence thoughts. Needless to say, you are doing your PRopaganda and telling stories, not playing Dante Alighieri, the Supreme Poet. Organize and optimize content to get the right PRopaganda to the right people at the right time. Craft it well but keep your message short and simple, depending on your final goal and your audience.

Deliver with intention.

THE MINSTREL

Ministration is the act of serving. There are many definitions of the Medieval European Bard, from middle Latin *Ministralis* to Italian *Menestrello*, or Old French *Ménestrel*.

The Minstrel was a medieval storyteller, a poet, a musician, a composer, a wandering singer, and much more.

Jesters were buffoons employed to tell jokes, and *Troubadours* told stories and sang songs of chivalry and courtly love. All of them were hired to provide general entertainment to the heads of Monarchy. There are no more Kings as Louis XIV remarking "l'état c'est moi" and in this new era of knowledge-intense and real-time information, we desperately need Minstrels.

Corporations, Media, Public Schools, and Governments took the king's place. A little élite, composed of few people, govern the masses, and you are asked to fit a rule in the society you live in. Nowadays, you have the power to tell your stories. We do need storytellers—people willing to stand up for something, people who do something, people who are flexible in their thinking, people with a curious and fluid mind, and people who change the world for the better (not the other way around).

Semantics is concerned with the study of meaning and life itself lives on it. Meaning is to life as water is. Minstrels were people who delivered meaning to their audiences. The plebs was all the other people in the surrounding. Plebs exist to date as storytelling modern Minstrels do. Plebs are all the faceless people who are fearful of standing up and defending their ideas, fearful of their shadows with regard to performing and delivering and more than ready to criticize and blame.

The modern merchant of stories shall be a *connoisseur* of the human mind and thrive on meaning, not being afraid of change and embracing challenges with a proactive attitude, performing in the best possible way, exceeding expectations, creatively finding alternatives in the face of adversities, and refining skills by exploiting every single opportunity to do so.

You need to be able to alter everything about yourself and your strategies by being flexible.

Be a semantic chameleon.

THE 4 PILLARS OF INFLUENCE

You must pay careful attention to the Context, the Source, the Message, and the Audience.

People are usually too busy and tend to fill information voids with whatever you feed them. That is the main reason for why it so easy for false allegations and gossip to spread. It goes without saying that credibility, authority, and trustworthiness are imperative. As far as the message is concerned, you should keep in mind that the main idea is to direct your audience's focus somewhere. You might do it by informing or educating your public and avoiding telling your audience what to think. No one likes other people telling them what to do. You should suggest what to think about instead. You might dust off a problem and offer a sound solution or a solution package that mirrors your desired course of action—vivid, concrete, personal, and fresh information that helps people to focus their thoughts. If people like you and agree with your point of view and solution, you're in game.

In a semantically loaded world you can design your message and even yourself (as the source) so that others will make positive inferences and associations about certain attributes of your website, yourself, and your products and services.

Envelope yourself with meaning. Disseminate clever information to influence minds.

People tend to persuade themselves and follow your path. They'll do the work for you.

INFUSãO

To my experience, the city of Lisbon is made of polite people. People at the *pasteleria*, bartenders, police officers and people walking down the street are all nice, helpful, and ready to smile. InFusão is a little vintage restaurant located in Rua da Trinidade. If you ever get a chance, don't miss out on it. The nice lady who owns the place told me that in English, *Fusão* means "mixing up." It's a fusion, a merger.

In the restaurant, you will find a little vintage shop, a nice selection of wines, the special dish of the day, and many *crêpes* (mixed up with all the possible combinations) as the traditional offers of the place. You feel at home when there. Your services marketing must be able to create this feeling in each one of your customers. Customers are then willing to do the marketing for you with delight. It is about what the experience means to people. Minds are made up of intricate neurological relationships between the meanings they created.

It must be a total customer experience.

A meaningful wow.

AUSSIES' GLOBAL HIT

The Global Marketing Campaign "There is Nothing Like Australia" launched by Tourism Australia became a Global Internet Hit. The marketing campaign and website were launched at the end of May 2010, alongside print and digital advertising, plus a video advert broadcast in cinemas and online—a four-year AUD250 million budget and digital channels as its heart.

This global campaign has received international industry recognition at the Pacific Asia Travel Association (PATA) Gold Awards and was award-winning in the overall marketing category and for its interactive website "There is Nothing Like Australia"—an integral part of the campaign.

As reported by several Aussie media, Tourism Australia Managing Director Mr. Andrew McEvoy is looking ahead to high-quality tourism and experiences, exploiting the power of the new media channels as a central facet to leverage word-of-mouse through the web. He also believes in the Aussies proudly promoting their land by sharing their favorite content as places and experiences with the overseas world—a critical element of the campaign's overall success.

The second phase of the campaign uses all the consumer-generated content to create an interactive digital map of Australia made up of things that Aussies think are special about their Country and attracting more than a million unique visitors each month. This is a super spiffy (*meaning cool*) example on how to exploit the power of the new media to engage people and attract visitors (not only to the website). The campaign's focus on digital advocacy to promote Australia to both international and domestic segments of the tourist trade led to an impressive response from the tourism industry. Domestic operators were encouraged to get involved and offered their own distribution and social media networks. As Mr. McEvoy said, the beauty of this strategy lies in its flexibility, and it becomes easy for it to be evolved to fit varied needs of the various players of the industry.

Things have changed a lot since the 1984 TV ad targeting America and starring worldwide famous Aussie actor Paul Hogan, known worldwide as Mr. Crocodile Dundee. Obviously, before the web came along and all the technological developments of the recent years, the only solution was to rely on traditional marketing techniques.

As Seth Godin wrote, *"Marketing by interrupting people isn't cost-effective anymore. You can't afford to seek out people and send them unwanted marketing messages, in large groups, and hope that some will send you money. Instead, the future belongs to marketers who establish a foundation and process where interested people can market to each other. Ignite consumer networks and then get out of the way and let them talk."* Outbound and Inbound Marketing channels do not need to be perfectly antithetic. Sure, interruption techniques are no longer tempting, but exploiting all the leverage techniques with a fresh mindset may still result in a great combination.

At the center of any successful marketing campaign, there is the public, the consumer, and the interested audience. Nowadays, it is virtually impossible to keep tight control of the message, and the best way to do marketing is to provide sublime meanings to individuals and masses and establish a unified attitude. Whatever the experience means to them conditions how they relate to you. Make it easy and cool for them to do the marketing for you.

Great marketing starts with the audience for a total consumer experience.

METAMORPHOSIS AND THE BUTTERFLY

Undoubtedly, we are a symbolic species and we live by symbolic domains. In many cultures, the elegant butterfly is often associated with the soul. In Greek mythology, the butterfly is depicted as Psyche, which, in turn, literally means soul.

The life cycle of a butterfly itself involves a remarkable series of changes, consisting of several parts—a process similar to ours:

- Courtship (like humans) to discover suitability of matching (*PS: And they do not use any online matching sites*).
- Mating to enable female eggs to be fertilized.
- Oviposition (Egg-laying process) takes place in a suitable site.
- Butterfly larvae or caterpillar birth.
- Ecdysis process (the caterpillar sheds its skin and grows to a larger size) in which the molt develops to a new instar (usually four or five times) until the caterpillar reaches sexual maturity.
- After this process, when the caterpillar is fully grown, it searches for a pupation site.
- Then there is the chrysalis stage (pupa stage of the butterfly) and the birth of the butterfly.
- When the process is complete, the cycle starts again.

Butterflies symbolize significant and sublime change. Life itself lives on change. Countless adaptations are said to be the bricks of evolution.

It should be a never-ending process, and we should learn to leave the old behind, as our passion for conservatism for instance, in order not to walk in circles over our rooted beliefs and traditions. Change begins within us by accepting our unconditional worth as living beings and being willing to explore life with a fluid mind.

It is not a temporary expedient. We metamorphosize any time we create yet another conceptual-meaning framework, transforming what the experiences in the real world mean to us.

Meaning is dynamic in its nature and changes all the time. Experience creates meanings, and meanings create experiences.

THE BUTTERFLY EFFECT

The term was coined by the pioneer of the Chaos Theory Edward N. Lorenz and refers to the propensity of a system to be highly sensitive to initial conditions. This was already discussed in literature, as French polymath Henry Poincaré found the dependence on initial conditions in a particular case of *the three-body problem* and later proposed that this particular phenomenon could be applied to other fields, such as meteorology, for instance.

Chaos theory is a field that studies the behavior of dynamical systems, a concept that finds its roots in Newtonian mechanics (Newton's laws of motion that describe the relationships between the forces acting on a body and its consequent motion). The idea that small causes might have larger effects dates back to antiquity, to the Aristotelian theory of motion.

Basically, all these scientific terms refer to the simple idea of minor events causing different and larger outcomes. Dynamical systems that exhibit properties ascribed to chaos are called hyperbolic systems. Nonlinear dynamical systems that exhibit a totally unpredictable, but fundamentally deterministic, behavior are called chaos.

Deterministic refers to systems in which future behavior is determined by initial conditions. Early states of the system determine later ones, but this does not imply that later states are predictable from knowledge of the early ones. Property of sensitive dependence on initial conditions makes a chaotic system largely unpredictable and long-term predictions fairly impossible.

This is different from the linear chain reaction that occurs with the Domino effect, where an event causes to initiate another. In a nonlinear system, a small change in a place can result in large differences, which might be unpredictable over time.

The popular notion is the wing flapping of a butterfly causing a hurricane's formation somewhere else in the planet. If the flapping of a butterfly can cause a hurricane, what can your meaning-making abilities do?

Don't you feel your innate sense of freedom of choice?

NOTHING ENDURES BUT CHANGE

We are a semantic species. We work with symbols and we live in a symbolic world of language and abstraction. To quote Heraclitus of Ephesus *"Nothing endures but change"* and *"You can never step into the same river, for new waters are always flowing on to you."* We live in a dynamic process world where nothing stays still, ever.

Change is depicted as to make the form of something different from what it is. Change is a natural process. Change is the norm. Obviously, there are two variables. We can direct our thinking and get ideas across to influence change or we end up influenced by it. In Human Nature, meaning is not a given. We invent worlds of meaning in our minds. We generate meaning and transform it into action. As Protagoras said, *"Man is the measure of all things."* "All things" refers to man-made meanings.

Inertia is the strongest adversary of any process. It is change's worst enemy. At this point in time, the ones who prefer to settle down are floating off the navigation route. A very high percentage of people on a worldwide scale finish school, do not even read a book after compulsory studies, get married, have kids, put on weight, and blame the society for not being as happy as they wish.

This is hypocritical, cheap, and lazy thinking. We are innately developmental, and we need to know what things are. We need meaning. We need to know how to live a meaningful life. This involves making mindful choices and taking ownership of our ultimate gift, the power of choice and will.

All of this requires meaning-attribution qualities.

CHINESE FLEXIBILITY

Italian fashion designer Giorgio Armani said, *"To create something exceptional, your mindset must be relentlessly focused on the smallest detail."*

There have been many technology advancements and a revolution in the way people interact. On the other hand, many companies are doing their best to stick with the old ways of doing business. Is it the fear of change? Is it the tight relationships that exist between businesses, scholastic institutions, and declining traditional mass media agencies?

In Milan, for instance, there are many Chinese restaurants. When the trend shifted to Japanese cuisine, what did these restaurants do? They changed the insignia of the place and started to offer Sushi, Sashimi, and Tempura. Many Italians are not able to see the cultural and physiological difference between Chinese and Japanese and everyone's happy. Chinese restaurants make a profit out of it, and people are happy to eat Japanese at a "Japanese restaurant."

Other organizations are not as flexible as the Chinese restaurants. They do their best to stick with the status quo and the false idea that "what worked in the past will work again in the future." This is an obsolete way of thinking based on historical facts. Many people hate change and are not flexible to embrace challenges. They fight against anyone who makes an effort toward change, trying to prove them wrong and declaring their thinking theoretically impossible and any future success unthinkable.

Regrettably for them, change is the only sure thing we face.

THE POWER OF THE CHOICE SHAPERS

Choosing is not an easy task. Your habits, your opinions, and your thoughts are molded by authorities and anonymous wire-pullers. The world we live in is operationally divided between nations, societies, families, businesses, religions, friends, groups of interest, teams, political parties, and so on.

Since antiquity, the collective masses tend to comply with the rules dictated by society—in other words, dictated by others. There are leaders (the director of the orchestra), players (the performers) and followers (members of the audience). The leader is also led by others—a few others.

Your thinking, your habits, and even your destiny have always been controlled by others. Since you were born, authoritative powers (family, military, public school, institutions, and religion) influenced your cognitive sphere and made choices on your behalf.

Despite the fact you believe to be the decision-maker, you find yourself in a funnel-shaped path. You buy a nice pair of business shoes but, paradoxically, you are not the same person who decided to market that exact pair of shoes to you. Why do you need business shoes? Can't you wear your favorite sneakers in the workplace?

There are rules and there are laws to comply with. I am not saying that you should break all the rules and start a revolution with regard to a dress code. I am just making a point about the fact that your decision-making power is often limited by others who already tailored a choice for you. The majority of people are happy with this. Most people do not like to research information and make sound decisions. They prefer the burden to make a decision to be on someone else's shoulders.

The news? Easy. Watch TV or listen to the radio or read a newspaper. The media never lie. This is another common stereotype that is rapidly changing. The modern media of communication make it easy for non-manipulated information to travel fast and spread around the globe. News is now fragmented and monopoly of information will not be regained.

At the end, it all comes down in your hands. Changing your old perspective and creating/offering your valuable and positive contribution to the world community requires a choice. But then again, it depends. Are you willing to be the artist directing your own orchestra?

Over time many said that knowledge is power. I would say that knowledge is a powerful tool that permits you to create new meanings that shape opinions and spread your word, your thinking, and your ideas.

Not someone else's.

THE CHOICE IS YOURS

Chart your way.

Decision-making is a cognitive process. It involves a selection. It involves a choice among two or multiple alternatives. The world is increasingly complex and problems are even more challenging than ever. The workplace is increasingly knowledge- and information-intensive and increasingly service-based.

The myth of cultural and mass standardized globalization does not seem to take place. On the contrary, diversity and hunger for independence seem to be growing. Attitudes strengthen under tradition and society, but these forces do not have the strength to suffocate thoughts and ideas.

Nothing can be done? This is just a cheap excuse. You have the power to do whatever you want, and, with the multitude of communication tools available to each one of us, the possibility of swaying public opinion is no longer mass media's executive privilege.

All depends on your decision-making processes. Your faculty of thinking and reasoning is endless. Why not create your own reality and challenge yourself by making your dreams real?

Selling yourself short is crazy and futile.

The choice is yours.

A PROCESS WORLD

The world is a dynamic place. Nothing is static. Everything is a patterned process, even your life. On the other hand, with regard to yourself, there are three categories where the crux of the matter might lie:

Reacting and responding to the events of the outside world.

Responding to expectations by filling a role and performing a script given to you in the social set.

Taking a proactive stance in life and making your choices.

Reacting and responding to the external world happens all the time. Unless you're a clairvoyant, it'd be impossible to plan or anticipate happenings in the real-time world of continual change that we live in. Reading lines and performing a script is the best formula to not enjoying life and going nowhere you'd like to.

Why not develop clear meanings out of your goals and do your best to create your own reality by making your dreams real?

THE GOOD CHOOSER

The power of decision-making lies in the fact that there is no black or white only. Aristotelian logic did not take into account all other colors in between. We can make multiple choices. Our mental processes are endless. We have the ability of representing the world in our heads, and we boast ownership over our binomial *thinking-feeling* patterns. Nobody can make us think or feel a certain way. You (and I) have the power to make decisions and to choose.

Clearly, this contains the asymmetric unwillingness to use this power. You can choose to stick with the status quo and be trapped in day-by-day boring routines, you can quit your job, you can get out of bed to go to work, you can stay in bed (and lose your job), you can wear shocking-pink socks, or you can decide not to wear socks.

Choices are endless even when you feel there's no choice. Some people are afraid of this power. Some are even unable or unwilling to make decisions.

There might be several reasons for this:

- The status quo is the easy way to go with.
- Fear of uncertainty.

- Fear of failure.
- It feels safe and it is not risky. Don't like risks.
- Not knowing what to expect.
- New is scary.

There are a lot of examples. However, it might be said that there is a common variable: a distressing and negative feeling dictated by not being able to predict the future, which may be translated as being afraid to be a decision-maker equals being afraid of the unpredictable future. Unpredictable consequences. The Butterfly Effect.

The past can hunt you down. The present is easily recognizable. What about the future? Predictions can be made, but there is absolutely no sure thing. This is the main reason for which people stick with a job they do not like, with a partner they no longer love, with a decision that felt to be the right one in the past but no longer is.

There are a lot of decision analysis tools that can be used in order to decompose a challenging problem into smaller bits (hopefully, helping you to find a great solution). Decision trees, sensitivity analysis, probability theories, influence diagrams, simulation, and scenario planning. These are tools—tools to help you to make decisions. Helpful as they can be, they do not make any decision on your behalf.

From the outfit you choose in the morning to the decision to merge (or not) with another company by investing billions, there is one simple thing to remember: the choice is *yours*.

Your entire life today is the sum total result of the quality of your choices, decisions, and meanings you made up to this moment. If you are not happy with any part of your life, it is up to you to begin to make different choices and better decisions. Your ability to set clear and accurate priorities on your time determines the entire quality of your life. Making well-considered decisions is critical.

Positive emotions have an impact and cause us to feel more comfortable in evaluating options and coming up with better decisions. The present is a sum of past choices while the future will be a sum of today's choices. Good choosers live better and are healthier.

There is always a choice.

CHOOSING TO CHOOSE

We make lots and lots of decisions on a daily basis. Despite the facility of making choices, when confronted with a problem, some people experience negative feelings, such as anxiety and uncertainty. It is argued that decision-making occurs as a reaction to a problem and/or alternative courses of action in order to decide the path to a desired outcome.

A lot of researchers agree on the fact that the optimal decision-maker is to be considered rational. To make rationally sound decisions, one of the basic rational decision-making models offers a six-step guide as a process of *defining the problem, identifying decision criteria* and *allocating weight* to them, *developing* and *evaluating* alternatives, *selecting* the best course of action, and *monitoring the results.*

The world we live in is increasingly complex, and, nowadays, it is vital to be able to deal with complex issues. If unaided, our brains seem to have limited capacity for coping with complexity. This is the main reason for which complex concepts and theories are to be translated into simple models, diagrams, or concepts that are easier to understand. In the face of complexity, we find it very difficult to handle a particular situation. We feel overwhelmed and frustrated.

Lots of decisions might involve multiple objectives, uncertainty, complex structures, and, clearly, unknown consequences. The key to solving complex issues is to chunk down the problem to more manageable bits. The decomposition of a problem into smaller sections is the very first step involved when analyzing a decision problem. Decision analysis tools will not solve the problem on your behalf. Ultimately, you are the person in charge to decide a course of action. You are the decision-maker.

Most of the time, we do not have enough time to make a decision. The decision must be made in the quickest possible way. No time to use models. No time for brainstorming sessions. No time for theories in a real-time world. When that is the case, we rely on heuristics—in other words, our rules of thumb—or approximate methods—to make inferences between our knowledge and experiences and the environment.

Heuristics are especially used when we have no time, or cannot perform an exhaustive search on any decision-related topic. We might apply heuristics to guess which is the best option, to recall how we dealt with a similar problem, and to choose a similar course of action or eliminate aspects to any alternatives that fall below our cut-off point.

According to decision analysis experts, the key factors that affect how people make choices appear to be the following:

- Availability of time
- Effort involved
- Knowledge of the environment
- The desire to minimize (internal) conflict with regard to the decision
- Need to justify (or not) the decision made to others

- Importance and consequences of making an accurate decision
- Implied meanings

I would say that, turning to ourselves, the main dilemma lies in what the decision to be made means to us. All our decisions are all-pervading with regard to our lives. Each decision we make has its consequences. Each decision can limit or empower us. The choices we make as we navigate through the world are strictly related to the interrelationship between the meanings we have created over time and our volitional power by which we make up our minds and decide.

The power of choice.

> *"When you have to make a choice and don't make it, that is in itself a choice."*
>
> (WILLIAM JAMES)

THE FASHIONABLE DEVIL ASKING FOR YES PEOPLE

> *"I pay you and you do what I want!"*
> *"I am the managing director of an international company, far too busy for listening to others!"*
> *"Do not ever answer back to me!"*

Nope, this is not the 2006 movie *The Devil Wears Prada* telling of a naïve young woman who went to New York and found a job as the assistant of the successful head of the biggest magazine in town, ruthless and cynical Miranda Priestly.

These are typical phrases you could hear during a working day coming from the MD of a company I used to work for a long time ago.

As you can imagine, the environment was overwhelmed with a collective negative mood when she was screaming around, or just around. She still wanted yes-people around her. You needed to comply with any of her requests outside working hours and late at night also; otherwise, you would be verbally abused and menaced of being "terminated."

Many human resource management and organizational behavior textbooks offer various definitions of leadership and management styles. My take is that it is reductive to try to classify everything. Managing people this way is counterproductive and meaningless. It reminds me of a phenomenon sometimes referred to as *Capture-Bonding*. The Stockholm Syndrome is a psychological yet paradoxical phenomenon. During and after captivity, hostages express empathy with their warder. They express positive feelings toward the captors and might even defend them. The captors somewhat acquire a positive meaning to them!

Contrariwise, as Machiavelli suggested in his political treatise, to maintain power, a man should take the right precautions, and his personality and style need to keep everybody in a positive state of mind. Over time, this solid foundation will result in people never letting the leader down.

BOOGEYMAN LEADERS

Many leaders of the past and leaders of the present enjoy playing with instilling fear and with the fact that, as individuals, we tend to exaggerate problems, doubts, and hopes. The fear appeal is a great human motivator. Abusive use of violent affirmation, arguments, and language added to outward scarce logical reasoning is a common characteristic of leading figures of the past. Leaders play on other people's emotions and profess dramatic consequences if their will is not followed.

At the Red Army Parade on the Red Square in Moscow (7 November 1941) Stalin said, "*For the complete destruction of the German invaders. Death to the German invaders. Long live our glorious Motherland, her liberty and her independence under the banner of Lenin, forward to victory!*" In a conversation between Adolf Hitler and Josef Hell (1922), Hitler was reported to say, "*If I am ever really in power, the destruction of the Jews will be my first and most important job!*" In front of the United Nations Committee, Bush defended the Iraq invasion: "*The commitments we make must have meaning. When we say serious consequences, for the sake of peace, there must be serious consequences!*"

Death, destruction, and dramatic and serious consequences aligned to commitment and victory. History saw many of these speeches. Organizations see many of these speeches daily. Masters and commanders instill fear and then offer their solution/remedies in order to reduce the stressed feelings they created in other people with the help of another instrument of PRopaganda: dramatization of personality.

Fear. Relief. Fear. Rewards. A devilish maneuver.

CULT-LIKE STYLE LEADERS

Ardent convictions add more intensity to the power of suggestion. A cult-like religious sentiment is manufactured.

As Le Bon wrote, this sentiment is like "*worship of a being supposed superior, fear of the power with which the being is credited, blind submission to commands, inability to discuss dogmas and the desire to spread them and the tendency to consider as enemies all whom they are not accepted.*" This is the intolerance and fanaticism of the Inquisition, the Communists, the Nazis, and, to date, terrorists.

Almost all the apocalyptic orders, satanic cults, and cult-like entities operate through religious terror merged with devotion. These secret sects are all highly leader-oriented. The personality of the leader is imbued with prestige, the mainspring of authority. As professor Pratkanis and social psychologist Aronson point out, the style of leading mirrors a punishment/reward boogeymen pattern, and communications are highly centralized. Leaders are often driven by fanatical passion and master the use of inflammatory rhetoric.

To become a cult-leading figure:

- Eliminate any other source of information other than yours.
- Provide your interpretation of the world and build your own social reality.
- Promise transformation and alluring concepts.
- Divide followers from outsiders. The latter are the unchosen. Create an Us-versus-Them dynamic. To avoid boredom and inertia, in case you have no enemies, invent them.
- Establish commitment via emotional tricks and traps.
- Widely use suggestive storytelling to manufacture your credibility and attractiveness as the leader.
- Build enthusiasm around yourself.

- Have members spread the word and fund-raise. The more they spread the word, the more they become self-convinced.
- Distract members from private, independent, and critical thinking.
- Keep control on members' thoughts.
- Play with the sense of time and dreams to fixate the vision of your promised bright, illusive future continually.
- Provide purpose, mission, and direction.
- Passionately motivate.
- Provide meaning.

One needs not forget that people have an innate desire to believe in something, and a well-crafted belief system can give power to anyone able to put it in place.

"To become the founder of a new religion one must be psychologically infallible in one's knowledge of a certain average type of souls who have not yet recognized that they belong together."

(Friedrich Nietzsche)

NO FLEXIBILITY WITHIN MILITARY-STYLE ORGANIZATIONS

Management is a funny word. It is semantically loaded with various meanings, and its interpretation really depends on the context. Revolution is more explicit; it comes from Latin word *revolutio*, which means "a turnaround." It refers to change. Change is scary for many, especially when it comes to any management context.

Communication devices and development in communication technology come from the military. Organizations were (and are) built around tight and hierarchical military schemes. Many managers act as lieutenant colonels with their people but are not able to lead. Internal communication is still top-down and "You, employee, must do what I tell you!" There is then a strong tendency to harden theories and concepts into dogma. However, the old ways of doing things need to be put behind. Superior strategists of the past saw things as they were. They were highly sensitive to the environment, to dangers and opportunities. That is what we need. We need moving minds—minds that are always excited and curious, determined and equipped with a presence of mind to keep moving forward.

The status quo and the comfort zone are dangerous places in war and in business. One must act or suffer the consequences of not having acted. This is the problem with organizational behavior: trying to do new things the old, safe, and relaxing way.

War is based on deception, whereas in business it is better to keep the word and promote quality meanings.

Dynamically fluid meanings.

THE APPLE SHOT

Wilhelm Tell is a Swiss folk hero. He was an expert archer with his crossbow. The legend recounts that Austrian tyrants, seeking to invade the (Swiss) region of Uri, raised a pole with one of their lord's hat on its tip in the central square of the village of Altdorf, and they required all the villagers to bow in front of it.

It was 1307.

Wilhelm Tell passed by without bowing. As a punishment, he was forced to take a shot at an apple positioned on his son's head. He split the apple. However, he also had a hidden spare bolt he would have used to target the imperial Vogt.

It is believed that Wilhelm Tell played a leading role in the rebellion that eventually led to the formation of the Swiss Confederation.

He was forced to target the apple.

Your stakeholders are not an apple. People should not bow in front of a hat. Your customers do not like to be named "targets." Meanings need to be altered for a better service.

The word *target* is no longer tempting in today's e-market world of ideas and meaning.

IT IS NOT MY FAULT

Coercion and fear are easy.

Much easier than proactively proposing new meanings and participating with creative ideas. Politicians are experts in blaming others. We are good at blaming others too. We are not so good at proposing creative solutions. Within a society that is not very tolerant with failure, our ego-protective tendency to over-justify leads to blame. The negative meaning attributed to failure would lead to catastrophic consequences.

Thereby, it is never our fault.

Wrong. We would need the ego strength and courage to correct and improve and to learn from experiences without attributing too much negative weight to the meanings we create in our minds. This can only be done if we have the strength to admit we were wrong, if it is the case, and use the feedback to learn and improve ourselves.

VICTORY OR DEATH

The aftertaste of winning by crushing one's opponent (Win/Lose) is a primitive trait of human nature. As a consequence, some deploy all sorts of strategies and subtle tactics for victorious success. The main problem with this approach lies in the fact that goals and objectives have the product/service (and financial results) as the starting point and do not consider the Win/Win basics.

The starting point must be the public.

The concept of strategy requires clarity of direction and necessary flexibility to embrace change and challenges to exploit opportunities. Armed with too many variables, it would be impossible to reduce the concept of strategy to simple magic formulas. Products and services shall be tailored to perfectly fit the customers' desires and wishes as a starting point.

It is not true that, in your industry, all products and services are the same. No two products are alike; they might be, at least, similar. True differentiation is not seen as frequently as we'd think. By departing from a simple statement "Business equals creating value for your customers," we can easily infer that the foundation of it all is to provide sublime meanings through superior service and exceeding quality expectations in a consistent manner.

Competitive advantage comes down to being truly different. Establishing a competitive position is about putting into effect tactics and strategies, with the ultimate goal of delivering a unique mix of value from a customer's standpoint and exceeding expectations—a total customer experience full of meaning.

Unfortunately, most of the time, these principles fall down to "me-too" boring strategies, pricing wars, and quality issues, which, in turn, erode margins and do not offer any added value to the end consumer.

Market intelligence is more essential than ever. Acquiring information and being on top of the news and knowledgeable are the very first steps toward the strategist wisdom.

> *"I never read any treaties on strategy... When we fight, we do not take any books with us."*
>
> (Mao Tse-Tung)

THE MISUSE OF FLEXIBILITY

In the interconnected, complex, and multitasking world we live in, a flexible attitude is much needed. On the other hand, the semantics of this term are often mistreated and applied as a byword for obedience, control, and discipline. "If you do what I want you to do" equates to you being a flexible person.

This is a very cheap form of cognizing that we might find within rigid command and control styles of thinking and organizing businesses. In the business arena, success comes from proactively and flexibly shifting toward developmental change, free from stereotyped behaviors of not being able to relate to the best asset ever.

People.

THE BOTTOM LINE IS PEOPLE

Many companies hire personnel and then menace them all the time as the fashionable devil does.

Initiative is not welcomed. Initiative is dangerous. Initiative is able to do harm, especially for middle managers and gatekeepers who are afraid to lose their chairs. The outcome? In a command and control absolute business monarchy, initiative is to be avoided, as if we were talking about Black Death.

Do companies trust their employees? Not always. Most of the time organizations' communication style is top-down, and if you are to be found *"down the stairs,"* you'd better keep your mouth shut. It is disrespectful to voice your thoughts. It is no good. It is evil.

This is a shame. If companies are hiring personnel, they should be able to empower them in order to exploit their skills and capabilities toward achieving the overall vision and objectives. This does not happen frequently. As a result, initiative is to be avoided.

Avoiding initiative equals missing out on intellectual creativeness and higher productivity and efficiency. Absence of a proactive aptitude leads to missing great opportunities. If it wasn't for people who take the initiative, we would not enjoy books, movies, nice clothes, nice cars, the wheel, great paintings, and great ideas. There would be no development; we'd be dwelling in a cave and, for sure, we would not be sharing content through the Internet.

A central facet of this current era comprises responsibility, proactive behavior, and knowledge.

Companies shall be able to empower their employees with solid meanings, and, vice versa, employees shall take responsibility for themselves. Business is a mental model. It is all about people. Behavior might be different depending on the circumstances, rules, and context, but, at the end, it is all about people.

What do you and your company mean to your employees?

BUSINESS STRATEGY THE IMPORTANCE OF PEOPLE

Competitive strategy is about delivering meaning. The ultimate goal of companies did not change: maximization of shareholder value is the primary financial goal and the basis for any strategy formulation. However, this new digital era of top-speed word-of-mouth and real-time information flow forces organizations to being flexible and adapt their thinking to a new mindset.

Marketing is no longer researching the needs and wants of the targeted segments of the market and pushing products and services through annoying and interruptive promo techniques.

It is important to define who you want to reach and be clear about what you want them to believe and to do. Todd Defren defined *Inbound Marketing as "being findability based on authority, based on authenticity, based on content, based on passion."* It is categorically imperative to offer compelling and passionate content to interested audiences that are eager to consume it. To attract your audience and appeal to them on an emotional level, content must have a fundamental characteristic: it must convey meaning. Meaning governs every aspect of our lives, especially emotions.

People go online for a multitude of reasons—to connect, interact, discuss, share, gather information, and have fun, complain, praise, and so on. Consumers decide. Business is done with and through people.

The bottom line of any business should be people (*internally and externally*), but often it is still the other way around. Strategies are still formulated on the basis of ROI, wrapped around products and services and overpromoted through the advertising machinery.

ROI is important but it is imperative not to undervalue the strategical importance of people, as consumers and as employees—one of the most important assets for modern organizations. Having the right and passionate people at the right place dramatically increases the probabilities of achieving any goal.

"Individually, we are one drop.
Together, we are an ocean."

(RYUNOSUKE SATORO)

HUMANIZING BUSINESS

Businesses exist to earn a profit from their operations. Humanizing is to imprint something with humaneness. Humanizing and business can coexist. There is no rule that says the contrary.

Consumers are asking for a corporate-human culture to develop. Organizations should revolutionize themselves each day—optimize processes, personalize their offerings, exceed expectations in terms of perceived value, work on building better interpersonal relationships, and improve their integrated communications with their publics. A united state of organizational mind would be a terrific marketing asset. Most of the time it is not possible, however; organizational dinosaurs are not keen toward change.

HOUSTON, WE HAVE AN ORGANIZATIONAL PROBLEM

The world is complex. People are complex. Organizations are made up of people. They are complex.

In this digital era, organizations need to be able to implement transformational change. Planned change is no longer a solution. We live in a new normality—a normality where dramatic and unplanned changes happen all the time.

There is too much emphasis on technology and not so much on people. Paradoxically, consumers are asking to be part of the game, whereas the corporate world replies with some technology and with banning social media and other web-related tools as they do with smoking.

The problem is not found in fear of change only. There are multiple facets to this freaky phenomenon:

- Fear of change and ignorance
- Managers who are unfit or unable to perform their duties
- No meritocracy
- Unclear understanding of motivation
- Command and control heart-failure attitude
- Managers primarily concerned with ROI and financial sheets
- No capability to solve problems and manage change
- No trust
- No collaboration effort
- Exploitative authoritative systems
- No leaders, just managers

A unified culture would be a tremendous asset.

THE HUMAN BODY AND THE ORGANIZATION

This is an easy metaphor. You know your body. The most complex organ is the brain and it sends out neurological commands to the entire body via its structure. Each organ is extremely important to the well-being of the whole, isn't it? The heart pumps blood, the lungs give you the marvelous opportunity to breathe, and the eyes? You can see. With your legs you can walk, run, jump, and dance.

Can you live without your left arm?

Yes, you can.

Can you live well without your left arm?

This reframes and shuffles your perspective, doesn't it?

Organizations operate pretty much as the human body does. It is very sad when gaps are too big and things go wrong as when top management earns benefits even when they do not accomplish their duties and do not give a dime about their people who might get fired in a thousandth of a second because of a quarterly report or as a consequence of wrong investments.

Take the Swissair example; in 2006, the Zurich Public Prosecutor's Office accused nineteen people on the company's administrative committee of the Swiss flag air company's bankruptcy. All of them were discharged and each received reparation between 80,000 and 500,000 Swiss francs.

Organizations shall be reinvented. We absolutely need leaders with genuine intentions seeing that most managers have not been able to demonstrate their acclaimed capabilities, neither in managing others nor in achieving the company's objectives.

The gap between management and workers is too big. Until you are ready to downsize your arms and legs and heart, your organization will not survive.

Winston Churchill said, "*The best argument against democracy is a five-minute conversation with the average voter.*" No one is pointing a gun at companies asking them to hire average and replaceable people.

MODERN BUSINESS MANAGEMENT

Eschatology is semantically depicted as being the predetermined course of events with regard to the end of the world as we know it. The world to come. This 2012 phenomenon comprises a wide range of eschatological beliefs and disruptive events that should occur on December 21, this current year.

Despite Doomsday theories, we might infer that we are already witnessing financial, emotional, political, and organizational turmoil pretty much everywhere around the globe. The 2012 business predictions are not so reassuring, and some companies have reacted by sheltering from the hypothetical and conjectural *and metaphorical* heavy rain.

At the same time, many are lowering their guards and turning their backs on long-term strategies; they seem much more interested in short-term quarterly profits and cheap hires to lower the major fixed costs and human resources. We live in a real-time world and there are now hundreds of new channels of thought to reach buyers directly. TV, radio, and newspapers are no longer the media. News is fragmented and social platforms are now regarded as mainstream. Why not lower traditional ad expenses instead?

Organizations shall stop to worship the monetary bottom line and be obsessed by it. If the only solution to summarize assets, liabilities, and shareholders' equity is to reduce costs by downsizing HR and materials and lowering service, you will have a great balance sheet at the end of a quarterly period, but what about in the long run?

Tech synergy is a must. Speed, agility, and a proactive attitude of each one of the employees shall be core, fundamental traits.

As are responsibility and trust.

RESPONSE-ABILITY

Your publics are vital to your business more than ever—you have a potentially universal audience. Employees are not less important and should be considered responsible and professional people, not costs or lazy people who do their best to avoid the responsibilities you are not willing to give them. If you think so, you might have a problem within the company you are leading.

Trust is vitally important in the workplace. Speed and agility and a proactive attitude are primary and basic rules within a company. Managing companies with the help of emotional trade-offs is not suggested in a knowledge-intense era that requires response-ability and robust sense of meaningfulness between humans—a unified human culture.

Be savvy with regard to technology and people and serve supreme meanings—the core ingredients for a perfect mix. Be outstanding. Be more than sublime by creating new meanings and exceeding expectations.

You'll be rewarded.

> *"Quality is never an accident; it is always the result of high intention, sincere effort, intelligent direction and skillful execution; it represents the wise choice of many alternatives."*

> (WILLIAM A. FOSTER)

FALLING THROUGH THE CRACKS

Thinking that prawns walk backwards is a common mistake. The innate escape mechanism used by lobsters, shrimps, prawns, and other marine and freshwater crustaceans is named Caridoid Escape Reaction. Rapid muscle flexion produces powerful swimming strokes to escape from predators.

The way many companies are structured makes it easy for procedures to undermine the total customer experience and organizational credibility. Disjointed operations and lack of effective communication between departments may lead to several problems in the long run. Customers might fall through the cracks of excessive bureaucracy. Sometimes, it is a good idea to step back and take accountability for the whole organizational structure.

Gaps need to be closed.

"Management is nothing more than
motivating other people."

(LEE IACOCCA)

THE CHANGING DEVELOPMENT MINDSET

On the US National Aeronautics and Space Administration's (NASA) website, you can browse to the fascinating Game Changing Development landing page: "*The Game Changing Development Program seeks to identify and rapidly mature innovative/high impact capabilities and technologies for infusion in a broad array of future NASA missions. Multiple performing teams using varied approaches will attempt to achieve selected high impact challenge goals.*" The program seeks to bridge the gap or, as they define it, the "*valley of death*" that has existed between a promising nascent idea and practical infusion in a space system. It is specifically designed to bridge high-risk/high-payoff technology from discovery to use.

Organizational development is primarily concerned with improving organizational effectiveness. Change is the norm, the new normality. Knowledge and skills are needed more than ever in order to build the capability of achieving key goals, solving problems, and managing evolutionary changes. Planned change is risky. Change is not manageable in advance. Authoritative command and control systems with big NO TREPASSING signs as their company policy with regard to responsibility and trust are no longer an answer to the market's needs, wants, and desires. Mass marketing and standardization is no longer an option. Mass media are drowning. The financial and economic downturn is omnipresent and will not go away so easily. Will the Euro survive? And the US dollar? Many questions.

There are few worthy and reliable answers to date.

The rules of the game have changed. A shift is needed. The valley of death between management and human resources must be closed without the downsizing, cutting-heads architect. You have all the resources you need to manage change and to be efficient, effective, and productive, don't you?

You just need to shift to a brand new mindset by creating new, significant meanings.

NO-NONSENSE CONTINUOUS IMPROVEMENT

We live in a process world. Things change all the time—by the day, by the second.

Military-style organizations with command and control management suffer in speed and agility of response. People need to receive orders before taking action. When they are not given the responsibility to do so, they must wait for someone to tell them what to do.

In Hebrew, *Krav Maga* means "contact fight." It is the official system of self-defense and hand-to-hand combat of the Israel Defense Forces (IDF), the Israeli National Police, and other security services. The system was created by Imi Lichtenfeld, and at one time, this knowledge was only available to military and law enforcement agencies.

In recent years, Krav Maga techniques have been developed to suit civilians. The system is simple and no-nonsense, and it is a realistic approach to personal safety. Its basic principles enhance individual instincts. In fact, we were born with self-defense reflexes as a natural reaction to threats.

The artistic logo includes letters K and M written in Hebrew. The two letters are surrounded by an open circle because the system can always be improved, whereas average and mediocre things can go out.

This is many organizations' missing spirit. Most of the time, companies approve some system (e.g. Total Quality Management, Six Sigma) and stick with it forever without changing or adapting anything to new needs.

Average and mediocre things can go out. Everything can always be improved.

TO INLFUENCE YOU NEED TO UNDERSTAND MINDS

Unless you find yourself being a hermit, either in business or in your private life, there is one particular aspect that is undeniably vital.

People's minds.

Almost everything you might need or want requires the cooperation of others. For this reason, in order to understand how people reason, make decisions, and construct meanings, it is categorically imperative to gain a basic knowledge of mind functioning, departing from yours.

As a preliminary remark, it is worth mentioning that Siddhārtha Gautama, commonly known as Buddha, said, *"We are what we think. All that we are arises with our thoughts. With our thoughts, we make the world."* He was right. Our thinking faculties make up our worlds of meanings.

Throughout history, many great thinkers tried to explain how our mind and body connection really works. Homer was the most important and *earliest* of the Greek and Roman writers. He is considered the writer of *The Iliad,* which is among the oldest substantial works of Western literature, and probably another work ascribed to him, *The Odyssey. The Iliad* recounts the siege of Troy and its (in part) sequel tells the journey back home of Ulysses. Astonishingly, in these masterpieces, Homer's vocabulary makes absolutely no reference to words suggesting any mental terms, such as thought, behavior, decision-making, belief, doubt, or introspection. These masterpieces tell us that, at that point in time (eighth century B.C.), feelings and emotions were believed to be located in some parts of the body—the heart, or often, the midriff.

Years later, literate Greeks at the time of Plato and Aristotle created a metaphorical space to house thinking, intention, and desires—the psyche—now commonly known as the mind. According to philosophy research, Aristotle's theories for the unity of mind are considered strong evidence against other beliefs that natural living wholes are like machines (mechanism theory) or the doctrine of dualism, which professes the coexistence between a nonphysical substance, the mind, and the body.

Jumping ahead in time, the scientific study of behavior, given birth by the twin fields of physiology and philosophy, added and reunited to the domain of neurosciences and other experimental techniques, helped to increase awareness with regard to our functioning and throw additional light on these issues.

Despite the fact that these assertions are far from conclusive, the main aim of philosophers to explain the relationship between mental processes and bodily feelings is still quite obscure with regard to scientific evidence.

NEUROPSYCH AND THE BRAIN

The brain is considered the center of the nervous system in vertebrate and most invertebrate animals.

It is argued that evolution took part in adapting brains to particular environmental conditions. This means that, to a certain degree, the brain has evolved over time in order to face new circumstances and solve problems related to humans' changing needs.

It is fascinating that this vital organ, which has been at the center of debates for centuries, is still magically "unknown" in its processes.

Mysteriously charming.

The concept of mind is understood in many ways by different traditions, schools of thought, and various disciplines.

In history, many brilliant thinkers like Hippocrates, Plato, Aristotle, Galen, and fast-forward to Copernicus, Galilei, and Da Vinci, tried to explain the relationship between mind, brain, and body.

It was not until the early nineteenth century that theories started to be focused on the fact that the brain is the organ of the mind and that different mental and moral faculties could be localized in particular cortical regions. This, as a reaction to phrenology, led to the study of cortical localization by other famous neuroexplorers, proposing several important discoveries related to language disorders.

The primary goal of neuropsychology is to use detailed behavioral analyses to make inferences with regard to the underlying structure and functional properties of the brain. At the same time, clinical neuropsychology is concerned with examining and explaining particular patterns of disorders in human behavior that might arise from disruptions in brain processes. Elaborate developments in the neuromedicine field offered a broader view of neurology patterns but failed to put scientific evidence on the table in order to contrast philosophy or religions' thinking.

Neuro-Semantics is totally different from the above and has now spread around the world. This interdisciplinary field of study takes place within a wider array of human sciences, and it is about creating and enhancing robust meanings, focusing on self-actualization for individuals, companies, communities, and nations and enabling them to implement the best values into actions to make up performance.

It is all about meaning.

CONCEIVING IN MIND

The word *thought* comes from Anglo-Saxon grammar and means "thinking" or "to conceive of in the mind". As far as the mind is concerned, it is important to grasp an important distinction—the difference between the conscious and unconscious mind.

A common illustration of this distinction is to think of the mind as an iceberg. The little amount that crops out of the water is the conscious, while the biggest underwater part is the unconscious. Conscious and unconscious mind are always present at the same time. But, we are not aware of both.

The conscious mind is governed by the left side of our brain. This part is considered being predominantly verbal. This is the part that uses logic and reason. The unconscious is governed by the right side and is in charge of governing the involuntary functions of our bodies and of being data keeper of thoughts, information, memories, and emotions. It controls every aspect of our physical being; it is said to remember almost all of our experiences precisely, and it might be regarded as computer hardware, storing many aspects of our past experiences. It is argued that conscious attention can attend five to ten items simultaneously while all other information is processed by the unconscious.

As Everett Dean Martin wrote, "*Only a part of our mental processes ever directly find expression in our conscious acts and words. The unchosen and the illogical run along with the desired and the logical material, only we have learned not to pay attention to such things.*" He considered "*attention as a spotlight thrown on a semi-darkened stage, moving here and there, revealing the figures upon which it is directed in vivid contrast with the darkly moving objects which animate the regions outside its circle.*"

We are not aware of both the conscious and the unconscious because, throughout our lifespan, we learned not to pay the due attention.

NO NEED FOR TREPANNING

Trepanning is a surgical intervention that consists of drilling or scraping a hole into the human skull to expose the Dura mater (the outermost of three layers of meninges surrounding brain and spinal cord) for healing purposes. Evidence from Neolithic remains from around the globe shows clear signs of holes of a smooth edge pattern in some skulls. This was practiced widely until relatively recent times in many cultures.

Many cultures seem to have used various forms of healing and intriguing techniques throughout history. The Greeks had temples of sleep (in which people in need of a cure would just lie down and sleep); other civilizations, such as ancient Chinese and Indian, are believed to have cured patients with words alone; whereas Egyptian priests would use a form of healing with their hands while patients were asleep. Furthermore, some kings were even credited to be able to cure others by the power of their "royal touch."

All of these healing processes of the past show that the power of mind and imagination were well understood by our forefathers. Nowadays, theoretical arguments in favor of more modern techniques, such as Electro-Convulsive Therapies (ECT), also known as electroshock, have not been stronger than Trepanning, with regard to healing purposes, whereas psychology and psychiatric teachings are often brought into question.

On the other hand, even though the skeptics scream at the placebo effect (because it works), other disciplines such as Neuro-Linguistic Programming (NLP), Neuro-Semantics (NS), Reiki, Chinese medicine, meditation, and hypnosis have gained ground in the Westernized lobbystic world.

The famous Latin quotation "*mente sana in corpore sano*," might be translated into the importance of the brain's role

Francesco Ferzini

in physical health and vice versa. Despite some exceptions, an energetic and fluid mind is only found in harmony with an energetic body.

Mente and *corpore* are to be considered a single entity.

HOLISTIC APPROACH: THE IMPORTANCE OF THE WHOLE

Cognitive psychology is a subdiscipline of psychology.

The term cognition derives from the Latin word *Cognoscere,* which means *"to know, to conceptualize."* This branch of psychology investigates internal mental processes, such as problem solving, memory, and language—in other words, information processing, knowledge, and human thinking.

As psychology disciplines proliferated throughout the twentieth century, many theories and models were offered that suggested numerous approaches about the mind and the human brain's internal processes. In 1890, Wilhelm Wundt, one of the founding figures of modern psychology, specified the senses, or the sensory system, as being the components of thought.

In 1933, Alfred Korzybski developed the theory of General Semantics. In the 1970s, John Grinder and Richard Bandler, made it possible to turn these findings into a brand new field of study: Neuro-Linguistic Programming (NLP). Later, psychologist and modeler of human excellence and self-actualization Michael L. Hall gave birth to Neuro-Semantics (NS).

Both disciplines accept the macro-level of the senses as the components of human beings' thinking. Research professor Candace B. Pert offers a perfect explanation of this: *"All sensory information undergoes a filtering process as it travels*

107

across one or more synapses, eventually (but not always) reaching the areas of higher processes, like the frontal lobes. There the sensory input—concerning the view, the odor, and the caress—enters our conscious awareness. The efficiency of the filtering process, which chooses what stimuli we pay attention to at any given moment, is determined by the quantity and quality of the receptors at these nodal points. The relative quantities and qualities of these receptors are determined by many things, among them your experiences yesterday and as a child, even what you ate for lunch today. Think of the brain as a machine for not merely filtering and storing this sensory input, but for associating it with other events or stimuli occurring simultaneously at any synapse or receptor along the way—that is, learning."

At our primary level of awareness we sense through our sensory system.

We see. We hear. We feel. Meaning begins here, with awareness and attention, by simply linking and associating the things we re-present in our minds.

We then create meanings about meanings, and the whole becomes greater than the sum of the parts.

INFORMATION PROCESSING

In our mind-body dichotomy, we have the power to gather and process information. Our brain is an information processor. We process information through our senses.

We see, we hear, we feel.

Our brain feeds on a great amount of information from the external world, processes all the data, and re-presents the data inside our mind. Each of us has a preferred sensory mode to represent information, and this reflects how our brains process data.

For instance, what comes to your mind when I ask you to imagine the following:

- The Sydney Opera House
- A mosquito flying next to your ears
- A relaxing bath with exotic vanilla-flavored soap
- Kissing someone
- Eating a cheeseburger

You are re-presenting information into your mind via your referencing points. You can see the Opera House, you can hear the mosquito disturbing you, and you can feel the pleasure of a relaxing vanilla bath in your holistic mind-body system.

You are making up meaning. This is what happens: we take experiences or information inside our mind-body system and re-present them. We can paint images, see pictures and movies, hear sounds, feel sensations, and even talk to ourselves. We internalize experiences and information and interpret them in a conceptual way. We associate experiences to our reference point for other similar experiences in our lives. By creating references, we also create meanings, and, by doing so, we construct a complex system of frames of reference and meanings— a complex cognitive framework made of thoughts from which ideas, values, beliefs and even emotional states are given birth.

A complex cognitive framework of woven meanings that govern our lives.

We are not machines and we were not born with software or hardware inside our heads. Initially, our brain needs to self-program itself until we are able to develop a constancy of representation. By learning and experiencing, we create frames of reference that become the reference points for future, similar experiences. We keep re-presenting things in our minds, and we associate and construct maps to help us navigate in the world. Thinking itself creates information and vice versa.

The choice of predicates shows our preferred representation systems and reveals a lot about us on how we see, hear, and feel the world. Awareness and attention occur at the primary level of consciousness, where we re-present things via our sensory channels (sights, sounds, sensations). Then, we link and associate things, and, seeing that consciousness itself is self-reflexive in its nature, we travel to higher abstraction and conceptualization levels to create new meanings about the meanings we have created.

Meanings arise from our thinking faculties, and the meanings we attribute to anything strongly conditions how we experience the experience itself.

External behavior and internal states of mind are strictly correlated. We connect things and we reflect back on thoughts and feelings as we layer up an abstract complexity, which is absolutely more intricate in its processes than the Semantic Web Layer Cake.

Depending on the context, once you understand how your publics preferred re-presentational system is, you have the possibility to craft your message and make it more appealing by conforming to people's preferred method of re-presenting information.

Have you ever noticed that if you show people what they are eager to see, tell them what they are eager to hear, and make them feel good about themselves in a consistent manner, they are hungry to spend more time around you?

They perceive you as being more attractive to them.

INFORMATION PROCESSING SHORCUTS

We live in a knowledge-intense, stereotyped world, and we are overloaded by tons of information that we need to process daily.

As NLP pushed the boundaries of traditional psychology, it became clearer that each of us lives in a unique world. The world we live in is a re-presentation of reality that we made up in our minds by processing the information we receive through our sensory input channels.

Our mind is endlessly creative. We create pictures and movies, we shape them, and we might brighten or condense them, lower the sound, or pump up the volume. We are the filmmakers of our own realities. The meaning-makers. This re-presentation of the real world helps us navigate through life. Fundamentally, we deal with a world that's well beyond our reach. There is a distinction between our universe and the real universe, and our experience of reality is not exactly the same as reality itself. It is an abstract, conceptual reality that may, sometimes, lead to confusion. Our perception of the world is just to be considered as a representation of it, not the real world itself.

Each of us has our own map of reality. Figuratively speaking, imagine a *Sat Nav* or a *geographic map*. If your *Global Positioning System (GPS)* or your *map* are not accurate and updated, you will probably get lost. The quality of our maps and the meanings we have constructed largely determine the quality of our lives.

More than thirty years ago, Richard Bandler was a young student and was asked to complete a manuscript of the Gestalt therapy's founder, Friedrich Salomon Perls, better known as Fritz Perls. Bandler soon discovered that there was some sort of magic spell in how Perls used language with his patients. Coming from a very different background than psychology and psychotherapy, he got caught in the structure of the language without being deviated by other theories on the subject.

Bandler, along with a young professor, John Grinder, started to focus on the structure of language used by Fritz Perls, family therapist Virginia Satir, and hypnotherapist Milton Erickson to discover how they were able to cause startling change with their clients while others failed. They cocreated the field of NLP by unlocking and proposing the structure of magic to the world.

The Meta Model was given birth. The initial model consisted of a dozen patterns of linguistic distinctions to enable a person to identify places of vagueness in the way one talks, which may create limitations to one's map of the world, and to uncover several recursive linguistic patterns on how language works and affects us all. Being a semantic class of life that uses symbols, words have a powerful impact on us.

Not to be overwhelmed and overloaded by data, we need some processes to manage information. The majority of problems arise when we delete, distort, or generalize information, creating un-supportive cognitive biases that might lead to inaccurate judgment, illogical interpretation, or perceptual distortions of reality. The model was designed to elicit more clarity and precision, and its linguistic distinction fell into three categories of questions that sought to challenge distortions, clarify generalizations, and recover deleted information occurring in the speaker's language.

Questioning has always been at the heart of the pragmatic model. The main objective is to separate what works from what does not work by questioning any ill-formed sentence in a conversational way, not in a police-interrogation style of gathering information.

Over the years, many changes occurred in the Meta Model as it was adapted to fields other than therapy (e.g. business, management, and self-improvement) and has been studied by many other researchers, academics, and professionals; it has even been extended.

The aim of the model is to be precise and meticulous— a communication tool to ask the right questions, gather quality information, uncover real meanings, and optimize life by communicating in a more effective way.

Deletions

Our mental constructs are quite limited in an ever-changing process world. When we delete information, we pay selective attention to certain parts of our experience by systematically deleting others. We filter things out into more manageable bits, screening out noises or deleting pieces of information when communicating or remembering something. We leave things out by omitting or forgetting.

Example:

When a comparison is made but the relation is not specified, this is defined as comparative deletion. What or who is being compared is unclear, and one needs to recover the deleted criteria for comparison.

Example: "You are much better at doing this."

Questioning: "Compared to what/whom?" – "Better than what/whom?"

Generalizations

We are masters in attaching labels and categorizing everything in the world. We generalize by applying a single rule (*drawing conclusions*) to each and every situation that might resemble the one in which we created that rule. We standardize. We always look for similarities. We summarize one or more experiences deciding that this is the way things are meant to be all the time. We represent an entire category on the basis of some experience—an Aristotelian black-and-white style of thinking that eliminates grey shadows and other colors in between.

As a consequence, our thinking becomes somewhat limited.

Example:

For instance, universal quantifiers imply that there is absolutely no exception to an experience. Usually, it is an all-or-nothing way of thinking. The need here is to explore all the implications of the generalization or to offer counterexamples.

Example: "All marketers are liars."
Questioning: "All of them?" – "Not even a genuine one?"

Distortions

Distortion is another way of filtering information. By deleting and generalizing, we shift the meaning of the experience. We distort reality. By re-producing, coding, and re-presenting information in our neurological systems, we distort things according to our own history and our own constructed meanings to make sense of things. All of us are inclined to distort reality for a perfect fit with our meanings, beliefs, and expectations.

Example:

Presuppositions may lead to distortions. They're assumptions about life, existence, and people that usually express unspoken paradigms in a covert manner. The need is to recover the assumptions and established beliefs in a specific way.

Example: "If only he knew what I had to go through."

Questioning: "What do you mean?" – "How do you know he does not know?"

As Richard Bandler himself suggested, it is important to get maximum information in the shortest possible time, so it is imperative to listen actively and to go for the biggest chunk to elicit quality information and obtain greater clarity in communication, seeing that we are too used to substituting, simplifying, talking names instead of objects or verbs, et cetera.

The key is to be able to ask good questions in order to gather specific intelligence—overtly and explicitly questioning to challenge distortions, clarify generalizations and recover deleted information occurring in the speaker's language to get maximum information in the shortest possible time.

How do you specifically know that you know what you think you know?

REALITY CREATION

Organizations play with information-processing models. Businesses want to attract, secure, and manage their publics' attention and awareness. They want their messages to be understood and accepted. They want to be associated with the very best and to educate and induce people to action.

To buy.

Massive doses of unilateral advertising messages to influence us are daily injected through the mass media. Mass media lived on the shoulders of a supremacy position for over a century. Every time we turn on the TV or radio or we read a book, brochure, magazine, or newspaper, someone is trying to strike our minds and have us act in some way. Everyone is trying hard to have us comply with their projected reality of the reality itself.

Persuasive attempts to influence by telling one side of the story work quite well because people do not have the time or the will to explore any alternative and blindly believe what that good-looking actor dressed in a white coat talking about teeth cleaning says. This or that brand is the very best in the entire world.

The authors of *Age of Propaganda: The Everyday Use and Abuse of Persuasion* wrote, "*The successful persuasion tactic is one that directs and channels thoughts so that the target thinks in a manner agreeable to the communicator's point of view: the successful tactic disrupts any negative thoughts and promotes positive thoughts about the proposed course of action.*" Lippmann made the same observation by saying, "*The subtlest and most pervasive of all influences are those which create and maintain stereotypes,*" and he said that any attempt to see things in detail and with a fresh perspective, without generalizing, is virtually impossible. Enlisting established points of view and preexisting beliefs is highly recommended when dealing with trying to influence the public mind. As Bernays wrote, "*Mental habits create stereotypes just as physical habits create certain definite reflex actions.*"

The easiest way to motivate people on how to think about something and influence their minds is to create images by directing thoughts to play on preexisting conditions, such as emotions, prejudices, stereotypes, biases, and other learned meanings to obtain the cognitive response desired.

As senior adviser to former President George W. Bush was quoted as saying in *The New York Times Magazine* (October 17, 2004): "*We're an empire now, and when we act, we create our own reality. And while you're studying that reality—judiciously, as you will—we'll act again, creating other new realities, which you can study too, and that's how things will sort out. We're history actors... and you, all of you, will be left to just study what we do."*

Reality is manufactured.

Created.

THE MENTALIST

Would you like to be able to read minds?

Sensory acuity is paying careful attention to other people and noticing their cues. By doing so, you are reading behaviors and understanding their sensory modes. As a consequence, you will be able to adapt to their view of the world, spot and use their language, and know their realities.

The only way that we have, as human beings, to perceive the external world is through our senses. The various senses play their role as information processors and are also known as *representation systems*, or *sensory modalities.*

The name of the VAKOG model (commonly referred as VAK) comes from the initial letters of the sensory-specific modalities: Visual, Auditory, Kinesthetic, Olfactory, and Gustatory. Highly visual people think in images, auditory people process the sounds of things, and kinesthetic people are into their feelings. This is reflected in the language used. We might pick up how people process information by listening to the word they use talking (e.g. I see, I hear, I feel).

Outside our neurology there are energy forces from which we pick up clues, data, and information with the help of our senses. Internally, we then process the data and create our meanings, our realities of the world. The images, sounds, and feelings in our minds (and bodies) are governed by the meanings we attribute to them and affect everything about how we experience reality itself.

One important premise is considered to be the foundation of the relationship between an object and the representation of the object itself. Our abstracted representation of reality differs from reality itself.

The map is not the territory.

Gathering this kind of intelligence means being able to know people better. By reading minds, you will be able to understand hidden meanings and gain compliance in the easiest possible way.

WE ARE SUCH STUFF AS THOUGHTS ARE MADE ON

Our mind is a neuro-semantic and holistic process of our entire mind-emotions-body system. We take experiences inside our minds, and we re-present them by associating and encoding and attaching meanings to these experiences and creating our abstract and conceptual realities. Everything starts from within the mind, and it is more important to understand how this structure works rather than focusing on traditional psychology's content-approach.

The first important concept is that you (and only you) are responsible for your own life. For this reason, it is extremely important for you to be in total control of your thoughts. Our neurological sense receptors pick information from the external world and re-present them, filtered and encoded, in our minds. We experience all kinds of thoughts at different levels. They might assume the form of pictures, movies, sounds, bodily sensations, and a wide range of other re-presentations.

In other words, we visualize things, we hear sounds, we feel sensations, and we experience internal dialogues with ourselves. Thinking and emoting do not perform their jobs on the same level because consciousness itself is self-reflexive in its nature. Much of our behavior is reflex-automatic. This means that we have the power to reflect upon our thinking and feelings. This self-reflexive process creates frames of reference onto previous similar experiences that run as reference points for individuals to make sense of things. To quote Bernays, *"Mental habits create stereotypes just as physical habits create certain definite reflex actions."*

The mental activity of thinking activates the center of the nervous system, and the most complex organ of our body sets into motion billions of neurons and signal pulses that give birth to a vast array of processes, from constructing meanings to emotions and to any other interaction with the environment. Individuals are the meaning-creators of the complex and conceptual world they live in.

It is worth noting that the brain does not function as our digestive system does. There is no alert system that sends warning signals when garbage gets in. The brain feeds on everything. As a natural consequence of this process, what you think determines the quality of the worlds of meanings we live in. Hence, your feelings, perceptions, and states of mind are your responsibility.

We could define our minds as our home, but, in reverse, nobody can enter it and steal our belongings. Neuro-semantic wisdom tells that we have the power to think and the power to emote, and nobody can make us think or feel in a certain way, except for the meanings we create and attribute to events and experiences.

History tells us that some people were even able to find positive meanings in the midst of extreme suffering and harsh conditions. This demonstrates that others can do their best to provoke us or evoke negative feelings, but, ultimately, it is an individual choice. This is our ultimate trench for freedom, our Fort Alamo—the power to think, to reflect upon thoughts, to emote, to speak, and to relate with the entire world.

This is a tremendous power available to those willing to take responsible ownership of their fortress.

Tremendous information to meaning-making architects.

SOME POPCORN, PLEASE

There are several distinctions to take into consideration when dealing with our internal representations. NLP makes two big distinctions, which are to be associated or dissociated (to step back). It might be we visualize things as if we were seeing them with our own eyes as a part of the scene, or it might be that we visualize things in a dissociated way, seeing ourselves in the scene as a third party. We have the power to play with our minds and to modify what we see, hear, and feel. Clearly, if we find ourselves in an associated state, we would experience feelings in a stronger way, whereas being dissociated helps to step outside of the situation and detach from it. It can change feeling intensity.

There are other distinctions of form or structure within a sensory representational system, commonly known as NLP sub-modalities (e.g. whether you visualize a still picture, a movie, colors, or black-and-white, and so on), but I won't get deep into those. Basically, we think in different ways (in pictures, in words, in feelings, in smells, and in tastes) and may break them down into sub-modalities of images, sounds, and feelings.

This is just to show you the magnificent power of our mind and to underline that we can easily play with it. The interesting thing is that you are in control and you can do pretty much whatever you want inside your head. You are not obliged to talk to yourself with a harsh tone when things do not go as planned, and no one will do you any harm if you step outside a frame of reference that you constructed and look at it from another point of view, reflecting upon it and controlling its quality to decide if it serves you well or if it is sabotaging you.

Sometimes, our mental constructs play against us. Perhaps, we believe that we are a total failure because we have lost our job. We might put into discussion our worth. We might get stuck with some wrong belief or something else. The wonderful thing is that all of this can be manipulated, managed, and solved. The most important thing is for you to be willing to run your own brain and take charge of it.

"Run your own brain, or someone else will."

(RICHARD BANDLER)

WE ARE NOT INTELLECTUAL PHILOSOPHERS

We are emotional beings.

Being emotional is a poetic faculty that leads us to personalize everything by somatizing our thoughts into our bodies. American writer Marya Mannes once said, "*The sign of an intelligent people is their ability to control their emotions by the application of reason.*" The fact is that emotions overwhelm our critical thinking abilities. We are not rational most of the time. Conditioned by the meanings we have created, we decide on emotions and then try to justify our behavior with rational thought.

Michael L. Hall gave a perfect definition of what an emotion is: "*The technical definition of emotion is action tendency generated in the brain (thalamus, hippocampus, and amygdale) as a response to some awareness (responses from mind and body that are not necessarily due to conscious mind/awareness). Emotions happen when we somatize the meanings of our minds and we might infer that source is our cognitive capabilities.*" Emotions are energy—meanings that we have created by somatizing our thoughts.

Many do believe that our behavior is still somewhat conditioned by the coding of our genes and our aboriginal nature. The Lizard Brain. A primitive form of behavior similar to animals that is dictated by a compact cluster of neurons, the amygdalae, located deep within the medial temporal lobes of our brains. The amygdalae is believed to perform primary roles in the processing and storing of memories and in triggering emotional reactions, such as the Flight-or-Fight response in the face of danger.

Aristotle defined emotions as "*all those feelings that so change men as to affect their judgments, and that are also attended by pain or pleasure.*" He found that there are fourteen emotions: Anger, Mildness, Love, Enmity, Fear, Confidence, Shame, Shamelessness, Benevolence, Pity, Indignation, Envy, Emulation, and Contempt. Our behavior is a consequence of our mental processes. We express our thoughts and feelings by acting and speaking. Emotions are also described as being intense feelings that are directed at something or someone.

As Candace Pert confirmed in her studies, body and mind are one. She explains that, in chemistry, a coordination complex is an atom bonded to a surrounding array of molecules or anions known as ligands. The body-wide info network is dynamic, flexible, and ever-changing. Ligands (smaller molecules than the molecular receptors they bind to) are divided into three chemical types: neurotransmitters, steroids, and peptides. Cells communicate and store information across systems. Emotional states are produced by neuropeptide ligands, and what we experience as an emotion or feeling is also a mechanism for activating a particular neuro-circuit simultaneously through the mind-body system.

There surely are dozens of positive and negative emotions that might vary in their frequency, duration, or intensity, but, ultimately, no one can make you feel or think in a certain way. However, stereotypes are strongly rooted in emotions, and the way we conceive, perceive, and interpret things is filtered through these biased lenses. Minds can be influenced by directing thoughts and emotions and serving new meanings.

Emotions are at the core of our being and our consequent behavior. The way you feel depends on how you choose to feel and on the meaning you attribute to experiences. Do you prefer to live in a dark world of distress and rage or in a fantasy realm of joy and happiness? It is your response-ability, your choice.

The most important aspect is that by attributing meanings we build beliefs. Sometimes we believe we are not good enough or that we do not deserve anything and avoid, as a consequence, living a good and full life. This is a great limitation and you should be fed up with any state of mind that contains these highly toxic and venomous beliefs.

You have the power to change these limitations and get rid of meaningless junk.

TRUE BELIEFS

Beliefs are thoughts we accepted and validated as being the true and real, either proven or unproven. Beliefs are what we consider as being the right and desirable courses of action. It is a psychological state of mind in which an individual holds a premise of knowing something to be true and gives commands to the nervous system.

Beliefs are different from attitudes, which are feelings about specific issues, and although often aligned to our belief system, values are what we hold in significance in life. The higher meanings of our minds govern our thinking and our lifestyle. Lifestyle is nothing more than how we live, taking into account our means, values, beliefs, and attitudes—our meanings as a whole.

Beliefs refer to the sense of certainty we hold with regard of some of our thoughts, and they are not easy to overthrow. Some beliefs are so deeply rooted into our unconscious mind that, when challenged, a strong emotional resistance appears. As a result, when you do firmly believe in something, you do your very best to prove that it is true.

Beliefs are very powerful. We all behave in ways that are totally consistent with our belief system. If we alter beliefs, we change behavior and vice versa. If we validate a new belief, we transform our behavior, and, by adopting a new behavior, we build additional information inside ourselves to adopt a new belief.

If you want to influence others with your PRopaganda, you might want to craft your messages around preexisting beliefs or challenge the source of beliefs by offering a wider range of possibilities or forcing the adoption of a new behavior. On the other hand, it might happen that the preexisting beliefs and the odds are against your arguments. Changing beliefs is not easy and telling people what to do is never appreciated.

You then need to channel thoughts by having your audience imagine and experience your desired course of action. You need to create a meaningful, bright, and imaginary future in their heads.

UNCOVERING VALUES INTEL

As you deem something as important, you appraise it as significant, meaningful, and valuable. You are deeply and unconsciously committed to what you value the most. Values are what we hold in esteem in life, and everything about ourselves reflects our meaningful values. All of us have a hierarchy of values that form our value system, a set of consistent ethical values.

Values are not static. They change over time, and they change from generation to generation. Values are what are truly important to us. Governed by the meaning we attribute to them, our values influence the way we see the world, and they are the foundation layer for understanding our attitudes and motivations.

What do values as pleasure, power, self-worth, self-efficacy, freedom, happiness, social recognition, and an exciting life mean to you?

Social psychologist Milton Rokeach developed a classification system of values by presenting the philosophical basis for the association of fundamental values with beliefs and attitudes, dividing them between instrumental and terminal values. Values, beliefs, and attitudes are the lenses from which we see the entire world. Your own lifestyle is dictated by these variables. Once we understand our way of filtering our experiences, it is much easier to understand other people's structure.

It has to be taken into account that values differ for each of us and, especially, from culture to culture. Never ever underestimate this power. What is important to you might be offensive or rude to others in the multicultural milieu. Once you know how the other person navigates through life (*beliefs, attitudes, value system, and lifestyle*), you are in a position of advantage, and if you are to wrap any request in the appropriate fashion, you have many more possibilities to gain compliance.

Values are fluid, not static. For this reason, it would be counterproductive to go by the book with the classification system of values. There is a much easier way to uncover what's important for other people: to ASK! Each of us has his/her own hierarchy of values. Therefore, the simple act of asking "What is meaningful to you in X?" elicits a deeper layer of thinking and triggers an unconscious response. If you were to ask "Why?" you would make a show-up-call to the conscious mind and get "Becaused" by logic. Why-questions evoke justification, explanation, critical thinking, and defensiveness. And you would get a meaningless reply seeing that people would try to justify their decision-making process and opinions with thoughtful and intolerant answers.

Remember, often people do not even know what they want, let alone how to give you a reasoned response.

"Only the man who crosses the river at night knows the value of the light of the day."

(CHINESE PROVERB)

VALUES, ATTITUDES, AND LIFESTYLES

The original VALS, launched by SRI International in 1978, extended into a widely used advertising and marketing tool. The framework, divided between motivation versus resources axes, has been widely used by advertisers and marketers as a psychographic market segmentation tool to tailor products and services to appeal to targeted customers and prospects. The main dimensions of the framework evaluate motivation (principles, knowledge, motives) and resources based on the degree to which people are innovative and possess resources (education, income, intelligence, leadership skills, et cetera).

As consumer attitudes evolved, the model was updated to explain the relationship between social psychology and consumer behavior. According to Strategic Business Insights, a team from SRI International, Stanford University, and the University of California, Berkley, determined that psychological traits are more stable than societal trends, and a new VALS was launched in 1989.

VALS segments US adults into eight distinct types—or mindsets—using a specific set of psychological traits and key demographics that drive consumer behavior:

VALS Framework and Segment Today:

Innovators are successful, sophisticated, take-charge people with high self-esteem. Because they have such abundant resources, they exhibit all three primary motivations in varying degrees. They are change leaders and are the most receptive to new ideas and tech. They are very active consumers, and their purchases reflect cultivated tastes for upscale niche products and services.

Thinkers are motivated by ideals. They are mature, satisfied, comfortable, and reflective people who value order, knowledge, and responsibility. They tend to be well-educated and actively seek out information in the decision-making process. They are well-informed about world and national events and are alert to opportunities to broaden their knowledge.

Believers are motivated by ideals. They are conservative, conventional people with concrete beliefs based on traditional, established codes: family, religion, community, and the nation. Many express moral codes that have deep roots and literal interpretation. They follow established routines, organized in large part around home, family, community, and social or religious organizations to which they belong.

Achievers are motivated by the desire for achievement. They have goal-oriented lifestyles and a deep commitment to career and family. Their social lives reflect this focus and are structured around family, their place of worship, and work. They live conventional lives, are politically conservative, and respect authority and the status quo. They value consensus, predictability, and stability over risk, intimacy, and self-discovery.

Strivers are trendy and fun-loving. Because they are motivated by achievement, Strivers are concerned about the opinions and approval of others. Money defines success for them, who do not have enough of it to meet their desires. They favor stylish products that emulate the purchases of people with greater material wealth. Many see themselves as having a job rather than a career, and a lack of skills and focus often prevents them from moving ahead.

Experiencers are motivated by self-expression. They are young, enthusiastic, and impulsive consumers. They quickly become enthusiastic about new possibilities but are equally quick to cool. They seek variety and excitement, savoring the new, the offbeat, and the risky. Their energy finds an outlet in exercise, sports, outdoor recreation, and social activities.

Makers *are motivated by self-expression. They express themselves and experience the world by working on it—building a house, raising children, fixing a car, or canning vegetables—and have enough skill and energy to carry out their projects successfully. They are practical people who have constructive skills and value self-sufficiency. They live within a traditional context of family, practical work, and physical recreation and have little interest in what lies outside that context.*

Survivors *live narrowly focused lives. Because they have few resources with which to cope, they often believe that the world is changing too quickly. They are comfortable with the familiar and are primarily concerned with safety and security. Because they must focus on meeting needs rather than fulfilling desires, Survivors do not show a strong primary motivation.*

Over the years, companies have tried every possible route to segment the market and identify groups of customers with similar desires and expectations using cluster analysis, such as psychographics sciences, combining psychology and demographics criteria to better understand consumers and appeal to their hot buttons. These models have been criticized as being too weak at predicting purchasing behavior, seeing that people within the same groups may exhibit very different behaviors. Furthermore, many of these tools are too national-centric (as for instance US-centric), hence cultural specific, and cannot be applied internationally, resulting in a poor tool for corporate decision-making and strategy.

Generalizing is dangerous and it may result in misleading assumptions to fix all your marketing efforts into these kinds of models. Behavior is strongly influenced by the social set but might vary amazingly from individual to individual, depending on the situation, groups, context, or occasion.

"Until we know what others think they know, we cannot truly understand their acts."

(WALTER LIPPMANN)

OFFLINE AND ONLINE BEHAVIOR

Since antiquity, marketers and sales personnel have dedicated lots of their time and effort in trying to understand what the consumers' motives are for purchasing products and services. Understanding what motivates people and then being able to push their right buttons is a dream for many.

What we know for sure from tons of research is that buying decisions are emotional, and logic is not much involved when people decide to buy. Fundamentally, we buy because we desire and/or we need. Therefore, triggering emotional responses is key to the process. Creating desires and needs is another way of increasing sales but can result in being accused of creating artificial values as has already happened in the past with several companies. It is well accepted that pleasure, happiness, and joy fuel purchasing decisions if compared to other emotional states such as sorrow, anger, pain, or fear. As a consequence, it is fairly important to trigger positive emotions when presenting problems and offering solutions. You need to be the clear alternative out of the fierce competition and be able to pull the strings of positive states of mind when offering the right solution to match the wants and desires of your audience.

Make it an easy and wonderful experience for others to do business with you.

It all lies in the positive meanings you create in their heads. Not yourself.

THE IDEOLOGY THAT MEN ARE ALL EQUAL IS WRONG

In 1937, psychologist Gordon Allport produced a definition still commonly used today: *"Personality is the dynamic organization within the individual of those psycho-physical systems that determine his unique adjustment to his environment."* In other words, personality is the sum of ways in which we react to and interact with events in the world and with other people.

It is a process.

Some personality characteristics are said to be caused by heredity and others by the environment (*culture, family, and social groups*) and situational variables. Personality might change depending on the situation. Early research and work in this field revolved around attempts to discover and label the enduring characteristics that may define and describe individual behavior. The Trait theory is a major approach to the discovery of personality traits, which can be defined as habitual patterns of behavior, thought, and emotion.

The Myer-Briggs Type Indicator (MBTI) is a questionnaire designed to measure our personality "luggage." Although it is widely used worldwide, there is no valid evidence that this is a valid measure. The Five Factor Model (FFM) is supported by various research, and it states that five basic dimensions are the foundation of all the other variables and wrap up the most significant variations in human personalities: Extroversion, Agreeableness, Consciousness, Emotional Stability, and Openness to Experience. Psychologist John Holland, arguing that *"the choice of a vocation is an expression of personality,"* developed yet another theory with regard to the typology of personality related to congruent occupations. The Holland Codes are divided into a six-factor typology used to describe persons in relation to their work environment: Doer, Thinker, Creator, Helper, Persuader, and Organizer.

As human beings, we are totally inclined to categorize and label everything. Categorizing is somewhat tempting, but we also have to take into account that we are all unique. We are not all alike. We are all different. Every day we wake up and move through our world manifesting the expression of ourselves in a multitude of ways. The way we behave, talk, do things, dress, walk, and emote are *unique traits of who we are.*

Categorizing equates to generalizing. Generalizing is a distortion of reality.

We do not *have* a personality. We express our personality through our actions. We learn personality, and, by learning and creating our worlds of meaning, we set up our mental lenses from which we see the world. Our values, beliefs, and expectations are governed by the meanings that make up our maps of the world and affect our sense of personality. As Lippmann wrote, *"We cannot fully understand the acts of other people, until we know what they think they know, then in order to do justice we have to appraise not only the information which has been at their disposal, but the minds through which they have filtered it."*

By discovering the sense of personality of other people, we can start to predict behaviors and, most importantly, become better communicators.

> *"As we grow as unique persons, we learn to respect the uniqueness of others."*
>
> (ROBERT SCHULLER)

PERSONALITY DEFINED

There is a great difference between static things and dynamic processes. Personality is not who we are but, rather, how we perform in life.

Personality is not a thing, either. It is a neuro-semantic fluid set of behaviors—a concept about a set of activities and processes that includes our ways of thinking, emoting, speaking, responding, relating, coping, et cetera.

Personality emerges from our functioning in relation to the environment and depends on context. We are not born with any personality. We learn the style of being persons as we grow up and keep developing our skills in various contexts.

Thinking, emoting, speaking, and behaving are at the very core of our nature and function as human beings. Primary-level experiences (primary representational domain of sensory-based language VAKOG) lead to perceptual programs and patterns that govern our thinking and perspectives on how we see the world.

Being habitual creatures, we do have our private style of sorting and encoding information from the surrounding environment. With our self-reflexive consciousness, we have the power of thinking about our thoughts and feelings. The higher states above primary-level states are layered states about states. As in the Semantic Web Layer Cake, the higher frame or state, governs all the lower ones.

In other words, we have an experience. We re-present it. We encode it. We evaluate and process it. We think, we create meanings, and emote. We respond to it in some way.

We all have our own strategies, based on how we have developed our meanings, ideas, psychic habits, and concepts through time. It is our way of being. No wonder we all have different styles of coping, adapting, functioning, relating, and behaving.

Freud thought of motivational forces as driving our behaviors. At the beginning, he wrapped his theories of people's needs and wants around sex. Later on, he added aggression to the equation. On the other hand, Maslow distinguished these drivers of personality as deficiency (survival needs, such as air, water, food, and shelter) and growth needs (security, safety, love, affection, self-esteem, and self-actualization). As neuro-semantic creatures, we strongly value these kinesthetic feelings (needs, wants, and desires). These energy-drivers are shaped by what we believe as being meaningful and what we seek to fulfill throughout our entire lifespan.

Over time, we build up our meanings-system, which is sometimes considered the difference between what brings us pain (illness, threats, et cetera) and pleasure (joy, excitement, and well-being). This way of explaining everything by a calculus of pain and pleasure is questioned by many. There is much more to the complex plasticity of the human equation and nature.

WHAT DO YOU REALLY WANT?

The word *personality* derives from the Latin word, *persona*, which means *mask*. The literal mask as figurative symbolism means something we hide behind when we wish to keep our innermost thoughts secret or, perhaps, when we are unsure of what we really want. We all have our fantasies, dreams, and desires. Most of the time, people do not succeed in getting what they want, and, often, they do not even know what they really want and where they are going in life.

Without action, our desires will remain what they are: worthless wishful thinking. The bottom line is to take complete control of our lives and realize that we are responsible for every decision we make. This is the underlying principle of outcome-based thinking.

We shall start every process with the outcome in mind.

This is the ability to visualize a clear and precise outcome of a process before even beginning the process itself. Our states of mind are undeniably vital to leading a successful lives and reaching our goals. Without clarity of direction, focus, and devotion to commitments, nothing will ever happen.

The idea of end goals dates back to Aristotle. He divided human motives into means (intermediate steps toward the accomplishment of a goal) and ends. There are various forms of smart goal-setting; however, it is argued that one particular aspect shall not be underestimated: writing.

Personal leadership is considered a process of keeping our visions and values aligned before ourselves and keeping our behaviors in life congruent with those visions and values. Writing down the wished outcomes of every situation is a powerful way to take charge of our own destiny. Taking some time to focus on what our life is all about and what we really want from it is a vital step in order to stop living a script decided by others. Our brain is an information processor. It does not make any decisions. It follows yours or other people's directions.

That's why it is strongly suggested to give specific directions to the brain and reinforce the meaning we attach to our desires by committing and writing things down. Goals shall be stated positively; you should not write down what you do not want because negative commands trigger and evoke the very things we wish to negate. Needless to say, you might want to create a list of goals that are under your area of control. If you never ever practiced any sports, it would be out of reach to state that your goal is to participate at the next Olympic Games. It is also a good idea to write down sub-goals, or smaller goals within a larger goal.

Have fun in the process and remember that a strategy without implementation is not a strategy.

"Focus on the journey, not the destination. Joy is found not in finishing an activity but doing it."

(GREG ANDERSON)

EYES WIDE OPEN DREAMS

We all live in a process world. Individually, we need a sense of direction and freedom of choice. To achieve any goal, we need either self-determination and, as the crux of the matter, the intentional will to be held responsible for our thoughts, feelings, and actions.

Canadian psychotherapist and writer Nathaniel Branden says, *"The essence of Self-responsibility is the practice of making oneself the cause of the effects of one's wants,"* believing that it is through independence and self-responsibility that people may attain personal power. This is the main difference between a reactive and a proactive *modus operandi.* Responsibility comes along with ego-strength and self-efficacy. It is all about trusting ourselves.

It is all about attitude.

Vividly visualizing yourself reaching your goals is a powerful tool. The value of *goal-setting* is widely recognized and accepted on a worldwide basis as a valid tool for achieving objectives. SMART is often cited as a mnemonic acronym, an abbreviation that helps memory to remember what it stands for with regard to achieving goals. Goal-setting involves establishing *Specific, Measurable, Attainable, Relevant, Time-Bound (smart)* objectives. Sometimes, two other major terms are added: *Evaluate* and *Reevaluate* making the acronym SMARTER.

The importance of setting well-defined goals is well-known by organizations, as the concept of strategy is. Agreed objectives, a profound understanding of the competitive environment, the appraisal of resources, clarity of direction, and the flexibility to exploit opportunities added to effective implementation are some key ingredients of a successful strategy.

We all live in a conceptual world. We all have our ideas, values, and frames of reference. We all have our talents and our passions. However, more often than not, a lot of people just sit down with the *status quo* and let life pass by, waiting for something to happen. Unfortunately, it does not work this way. Nothing happens by chance. Let's imagine top executives, the best athletes, and successful people. They all have some common traits. They all have clear objectives in mind, they all work hard, and they put great effort and passion in what they do. They did not find themselves where they are just by chance. Passion brought them there.

It all starts with designing a well-formed outcome in our mind. Pretty much as the SMART acronym tells us, we do need to state positive goals that lie within our areas of control. (Negation is considered as a disempowering command, and, clearly, hypothetically unrealistic goals will not serve you well.) Our brains need to be fed with specific directions. Our brains need to know where to go and what to do; they do not decide by themselves. We need to vividly imagine our objective, contextualize it, and define all the needed details on how to get there in the best possible way in order to exploit opportunities.

Precision, flexibility, and clarity of thought are vital ingredients for getting from A (*our present situation*) to B (*our objective*). It would be worthless to have a dream and not be willing to get there just because of a lack of willpower. Implementation is key to strategy. One needs to highly value his/her own goal(s) and attach meaning to objectives—passionate desire *plus* a go-for-it attitude.

Some things might not work. No one ever said it is going to be a piece of cake. On the other hand, if you drive off the road, try another way. If there are any setbacks, consider them as opportunities to learn and keep going with a "*never-surrender*" attitude.

We are often distracted and do not focus enough on what we are doing and where we are going in life. The solution is to commit and be very specific with regard to your desired outcomes in any situation. Have a dream, have a plan. Go for it and be persistent. Do not give up until you reach your objective. Be oriented toward action and making things happen. It takes total energy and strength concentrated toward your goal.

> "*You can't cross the sea merely by standing*
> *and staring at the water.*"
>
> (Rabindranath Tagore)

CATEGORICAL IMPERATIVE

Time management enables you to control the sequence of events in your life. Although we are used to giving precedence to a misconception of time (the twelve-month cycle of the Gregorian calendar paced by the clock is a human-crafted law), the meanings we map about time greatly influence our lives.

It is extremely easy to find legitimate reasons for not doing something. The most silly excuse is often "I have no time to do it."

Wrong.

As human beings, we're all masters when it comes down to making up excuses. Masters of lies. We now live in a post-industrial era where time has become a very scarce commodity—scarcer than ever in human history.

As a consequence, we are obliged to use this precious commodity wisely. We must manage it well and shift our attention and awareness where it deserves to be.

No wasting time allowed.

Complaining is no remedy.

Prioritizing, being determined, being motivated, and focusing are categorically imperative as the central facets of the philosophical concept developed by Immanuel Kant.

There are always choices. There is always time.

PRIORITIZING IN A MULTITASKING WORLD

The rapid tech developments, the rise of the modern media, and the real-time multitasking demands of today's life require the ability to focus and to prioritize tasks.

The new communication tools are extremely helpful; however, the possible downturn lies in infobesity and continuous interferences with what you are doing. This needs to be managed in the best possible way in order to accomplish any task or goal.

Lack of ability to pay attention or lack of interest in the object of attention does not permit a brilliant performance.

The task you are performing requires your total attention and determination.

Once you have given priority to something, your main duty is to focus.

THERE IS NO ULTIMATE SATISFACTION

Back in 1943, to understand what really drives people, psychologist Abraham Maslow proposed a fascinating theory in his research paper entitled "A Theory of Human Motivation." Maslow believed that there was not a good behavioral definition of motivation, seeing that historical theories on motivation were united in dividing, rejecting, or accepting impulses with regard to pain or pleasurable outcomes. He divided human needs into basic survival needs and higher ones.

The hierarchy of human needs, often portrayed as a pyramidal structure, has since then been studied in several fields, such as psychology, marketing, business, and economics. This psychological theory has been represented in various formats, sometimes criticized, and even further developed.

As human beings, we are a needy species, and we are restless in terms of developing. However, for complete human development to take place, we shall—unavoidably—follow the path of gratifying our lower needs all the way up toward the top of the pyramid.

It is argued that lower needs operate by deficiency and that the *puissant* drive to gratify the need dissolves when the need itself is gratified. Higher needs are not driven by shortages. They are desire-driven. Some needs are dependent on the environment, are deficiency-driven, and can be satisfied only by other people, whereas other needs are determined by our inner side rather than our social side.

Maslow argued against the Aristotelian logic that says that "*A is A and everything else is not A and never the twain shall meet.*" He viewed human beings as complete, whole individuals and considered as a single principle that binds together the multiplicity of human motives the tendency for new and higher needs to emerge when lower needs fulfilled and gratified.

All the pyramid's levels, being organized into a hierarchy, determine the fundamental nature of our motivational life. The lower needs operate by deficiency and are powerful drives (until the need is gratified), whereas the higher needs operate in a different way being considered growth drives toward actualizing our highest potentials. Beginning from lower needs (survival: food, water, shelter, and sex) to safety, social, and self-regard needs, we move up levels, depending on the meaning we attach to those needs. Without meaning, needs are just instincts. We are innately developmental.

Survival: This is the very basic prerogative for us all to function—a physiological need. We need food, and we need water for our bodies (and minds) to live. We have a sex drive for our species to reproduce.

Safety: Security is undoubtedly very important for us all with regard to personal, financial, or even health issues.

Social: We all wish for a sense of belonging—for love, affection, and acceptance in the society we live in.

Esteem, Self-Regard, Status: The acceptance of our self. As human beings, we feel the need and desire of being respected and valued.

Self-Actualization: This is considered as being a desire. It is not driven by deficiency. Basically, it does not mean being (or becoming) a super hero; it describes a way of being fully human—an ordinary man with no secret powers over others, but with nothing taken away, a fully human individual. Self-actualizing means becoming everything we already have the potential to become. It means making our passions and our talents actual and real [Potential Aesthetics: order, beauty and Cognitive/Meaning: knowledge, understanding].

Maslow's step-like structure assumes that lower needs need to be gratified before moving up the pyramid toward Self-Actualization. He argued that we might accept or reject driving impulses on the basis of past experience and/or expected future gratification.

A great deal of interest is put into the human needs theory. Social psychologists, researchers, marketers, sales professionals, and business schools are more than interested in trying to understand what motivates people.

The reason is simple: if you understand motives, you understand what drives and induces people to act.

MENTALLY SCREWED UP

Born on the roots of the past, traditional psychology and psychiatry have always been focused on healing what is considered to be broken. It is not by chance that there are many volumes like *the Diagnostic and Statistical Manual of Mental Disorders* (DSM), published by the American Psychiatric Association to provide standardization for the classification of mental disorders.

The Human Potential Movement (HPM) began to take form in the '50s and erupted out of the social and intellectual milieu of the '60s, creating new premises and fervor to change the rules in the psychology arena. Focused on actualizing human potential at its best, the movement was known as *"Third Force" in psychology*, after Freud's psychoanalysis and behaviorism, and established by J. Watson and B.F. Skinner. Advertisers were quick to apply the teaching of behaviorism to improve the effectiveness of their messages by repeatedly associating stimuli and exploiting psycho-analytics to appeal to the deepest human motives. However, the founding fathers of the movement did not agree on the fact that people were just driven by Pavlovian conditioning theories or Freudian assumptions that man is naturally antisocial, sex driven, and aggressive. Instead, they believed human nature to be driven by positive intentions, creativity, and willingness to take responsibilities toward higher meanings. The movement entered the scene revolutionizing traditional psychology's theories by considering the brightest aspects of human nature and potential, and by shifting its focus from broken and traumatized people to healthy and fully functioning human beings. The core model at the heart of HPM was Maslow's hierarchy of needs.

Along with Maslow, many others contributed their ideas and theories in identifying key concepts and analyzing other important aspects, such as meaning and personal responsibility, from the area of humanistic existentialism. In the same era, where psychology had come to be dominated by behaviorism and learning theories, American linguist Noam Chomsky created the transformational grammar model, proposing that most of our linguistic knowledge is innate. Transformational grammar revolutionized linguistics and launched the Cognitive revolution, defeating behaviorism.

In 1960, G. Miller, *author of the famous paper* "The Magical Number Seven, Plus or Minus Two: Some Limits on Our Capacity for Processing Information,*" along with E. Galanter and K. Pribram, proposed a "thinking strategy" based on feedback loops that behaviorists always considered unthinkable: the T.O.T.E Model (Test-Operate-Test-Exit)—an iterative problem-solving strategy.

In the meantime (1962), with a spiritual focus and the goal of bringing the Eastern philosophies and religions to the West, the Esalen Institute was opened at Big Sur in California.

Esalen started as a growth center where all kinds of processes were experimented.

It became the HPM base.

TOO ABSTRACT TO EXIST?

The HPM "school of thought" never became a school. It was widely criticized as being too abstract, individualistic, and narcissistic and as not delivering on its promises. It was not recognized as a philosophy of science, either. This might be due to a variety of reasons, which could be related to the tempers of the sixties and seventies in the United States (drug culture, anti-war, and establishment culture) or the willingness to maintain the lobbystic status quo.

According to Michael L. Hall, theories were vaguely proposed with no scientific well-formed language, and no specific methodologies were provided as a central effective model. Self-actualization concepts were somewhat confused with therapy and healing, and the strong emphasis on individualism did not make it possible for the movement to flourish. The fact that the experiments went from psychodrama to hypnosis and psychedelic-altered states led to a negative association with drugs and the counterculture.

The movement did not self-actualize.

"Dream in a pragmatic way."

(ALDOUS HUXLEY)

WHAT MOTIVATES YOU?

In most textbooks, motivation is defined as a driving force that accounts for the intensity, direction, and persistence of effort by which we move toward attaining our goals.

With regard to organizations, management professor Douglas McGregor examined theories of individual behavior at work and formulated two distinct assumptions of the average human being. Theory X assumes that people are lazy, they dislike working, and they are not keen to accept responsibility. Theory Y assumes that people like working, they seek responsibility, they are creative, and they can even exercise self-direction. Unfortunately, most organizations follow the X path, which is all about distrust, ignorance, and a very distorted view of human nature.

Many researchers further developed Maslow's hierarchy of needs. Most of them agree that the main problem of the pyramidal structure is found in its stiffness. It is static.

American psychologist Clayton Alderfer revised the hierarchy of needs and argued that there are three groups of core needs, proposing the ERG theory: Existence (providing basic material existence requirements), Relatedness (desire to maintain important interpersonal relationships), and Growth (intrinsic desire for growth and development). The ERG theory argues that more than one need might be operative at the same time, and in case the gratification of a higher need is "blocked," the desire to satisfy a lower-level need increases.

American psychological theorist David McClelland offers yet another theory and focuses on three other needs: For Achievement (drive to excel, drive to succeed), For Power (the need to make others behave in a way they would have not otherwise), For Affiliation (desire for friends and close relationships).

Without doubt, these theories —proposed by eminent and outstanding people—are more than valid, but, at the same time, they do not add strong evidence to the pyramid to answer the following questions.

What motivates people to do something? How do people reason and interpret things? What really drives people?

LIVING A MOTIVATION LIFE

Freud was obsessed by sex. He attached to sex extreme importance and he even invented new nomenclature: Libido. His view of human beings was that we are driven by sex impulses. He later slightly modified his beliefs by adding aggressiveness to the formula.

Other psychologists and researchers of his time fully embraced many of his ideas but argued on his thinking with regard to the importance of sexual motivation. Some proposed that the will to live is the greatest human motivator (Carl Gustav Jung), others thought about superiority and power (Alfred Adler), Carl Rogers said that people are driven by self-actualization, and Maslow argued that we are a needy species and that we always want something.

Adler broke away from Freud's negative deterministic view and focused on the importance of meaningful goals. Jung, as well, contemplated that the mind lives by aims. Organizations and academics have always been interested in understanding motivation. Motivation and human drives are obviously important for either purchasing decisions or employees' higher/better performance in the workplace.

At a business level, organizations tried all the possible ways to increase their staff motivation and performance by putting into practice programs consisting in personal attention, interest, approval, and appreciation for a job well done, as management by objectives, employee recognition programs, employee involvement programs, participative management, and many others, like quality circles meetings, benefit plans, flexible spending plans, et cetera.

All these approaches might be considered valid, but the absence of problems and criticism has been impossible due to the fact that seniors often align with the traditional autocratic style of managing the workforce—there might be different levels of expertise and background and, most importantly, not everyone is motivated by the same needs, wants, and desires.

Globalization led to a more diversified and mobile workforce, surfacing the need of understanding and responding to diversity in an even more flexible way. Once you know what people's motives are, you can easily influence minds.

Knowing what motivates you is key to changing your own behavior and is a first step to better understanding your public.

LEADERS AND MANAGERS ARE NOT EXACTLY THE SAME

Leadership is often depicted as an influence process that clearly encompasses other inevitable variables, from trust to liking. Leaders are re-framers, meaning shapers. Charisma is a transformational characteristic and may lead to devout followers transcending their self-interests.

The common trait seems to be that these people are masters in attracting people to their side. There is a profound and cult-like effect on people who are hypnotized by the meaning-masters, considered as information-keepers, who have the power to disseminate and propagate their word or conceal and even censor information.

Effective managers must develop leadership qualities and give evidence of their capabilities to perform their jobs. Paradoxically, the hierarchical and military "command and control" style of management does not leave any chance for a manager to be (or become) a leader. Many too-formal organization charts do not permit any rotation of responsibilities. Hence, it becomes quite tricky when it comes to empowering people, seeing that important roles, such as coaching and mentoring, are often forgotten. Command and control freaks do not trust other people and are incapable of delegating. Consequently, their middle managers cannot afford to empower others.

Although there are big differences between leaders and managers and all can be strongly influenced by the cultural environment, the leader shall be able to do the following:

- Create a vision and set the direction.
- Be the meaning-shaper and architect.
- Inspire others by aligning them to the vision.
- Be a passionate agent of change.
- Be a skilled facilitator, coach, and mentor (empower others).
- Be a synergizer with a proactive and positive attitude.
- Motivate with driving passion and unify attitudes.

Managers shall complete this process by efficiently and effectively organizing, planning, and controlling all the available resources. Their primary duty is to translate the vision into reality. Behaviors that lead to being hated or held in contempt as the fashionable devil should be avoided to create a congruent and authentic meaning for employees.

Understanding how people create their worlds of meaning is a vital remedy to failure.

THE KING OF THE JUNGLE

What do food, sex, and shelter mean to you?

Shelter, sex, and food hunger are the universal human self-preservation instincts. Survival is one of our greatest motivators. Human nature research clearly demonstrates that there are few basic drives that are critical for our survival: Food (and water), Reproduction (sex), and the ability to flee or fight in the face of dangerous situations. In our modern societies, everyone positively responds to the most basic appeals for shelter, food, amusement, beauty, and romance, and this is the major reason for capitalizing these fundamental needs through clever appeals to universal desires and instincts.

Appealing to the need for food is quite critical. In Far East Asia, for example, deals are closed at lunch or dinner. Trust is gained over the same time. Food is important—vital.

The very act of sex, romance, and flirting is innate in humans. The desire for romance is a powerful motivator, and many organizations, from fashion companies to hair dressers and beauty specialists, all gain from appealing to these needs. All of us want to be perceived as attractive by others.

Fear is another important drive. We are so conditioned by the amygdalae and by our prehistoric nature that we behave in various ways when faced with danger. Our stimulus-response Lizard Brain activates our deepest warning and safeguard mechanism, and we react to impulse by fleeing or fighting.

We are self-centered and egoistical as individuals. This is reflected by the social set mirror. Evolutionary psychology theories talk about jungle-style behavior, so why not appeal to social ladder advantages and gains when trying to influence minds? No matter the media highways and channels of thought, any public will always respond to these basic appeals and to a leading authority.

SIXTEEN BASIC DESIRES

Extending Maslow's thinking, who said that the new experience validates itself rather than being validated by any outside criterion or by being self-justifying and validating, we discover the philosophical ultimate questions:

What am I?

Who am I?

Dr. Steven Reiss made an interesting attempt to categorize and segment people to understand human motives and drives. He argues that, because of genetic variations in our basic desires, no two people enjoy the same experience in the same way. Human motives are complex and modified by culture, experiences, beliefs, and values. Any difference in our basic desires might lead to miscommunication, misunderstandings, and conflict. According to his scientific research, there are sixteen basic desires that drive much of human behavior. Every desire creates an opposite desire, and the experience has a subjective/relative importance, depending on the intensity of the feeling and importance attached to it. The following are the sixteen basic desires:

- POWER: The desire to influence the behavior of others.
- INDEPENDENCE: Desire for self-reliance and freedom.
- CURIOSITY: Desire for knowledge.
- ACCEPTANCE: Desire for social inclusion.
- ORDER: Desire for organization and control.
- SAVING: Desire to collect things. Ant or Squirrel?
- HONOR: Desire to be loyal to one's parents, heritage, and tradition.
- IDEALISM: Desire for social justice. Ideology.
- SOCIAL CONTACT: Desire for companionship.
- FAMILY: Desire to raise one's own children.

- STATUS: Desire for social standing. To be perceived as important.
- VENGEANCE: Desire to get even.
- ROMANCE: Desire for sex, beauty, and romance.
- EATING: Desire to consume food.
- PHYSICAL ACTIVITY: Desire for exercise of muscles. To be physically fit.
- TRANQUILLITY: Desire for emotional calm.

As for the VALS model, this interesting research would need to be expanded to the entire globe seeing that it is considered to be too culture-centric being executed only on specimens from America, Canada, and Japan.

A naïve aspect might lie in the idea that human behavior can be assessed in relation to a set of desires expressed by a sample of people because behavior not only depends on the intensity of the feelings and importance, but rather on the meanings attached to it and the uniqueness of the individual.

What people consider as being important and valuable is not to be considered a static psychological trait. Too many stereotypes and generalizations might be drawn from statistically chosen samples. Human qualities are too vague and opaque and, respectively, too dynamic and fluctuating to be classified.

It is a dynamic process—a process made up of preconceptions and ever-changing meanings.

SELF-ACTUALIZATION

Everyone wants to live a good life. Self-actualization is being fully human. It means living a playful, enriching, explorative, and meaningful life.

There is one thing on which everyone agrees; Maslow's pyramid shall be seen as fluid and not as a static model. As Michael L. Hall and other experts argue, Maslow essentially left out an incredibly important and critical dimension of our intrinsic human nature. He did not to take into account our fluid nature and how the meanings we create attribute value to our needs.

Hall reminds that needs are subjective and quite relative in their shape; everything is to be seen as fluid and does not stop with the top end of Maslow's pyramidal structure. Maslow said, *"What a man can be, he must be."* We are inherently restless, and there is no ultimate satisfaction.

Self-actualization is concerned with making our talents, passions, potentials, and dreams come true—being an ordinary person with nothing taken away and rediscovering the beauty of being fully human. From Maslow's hierarchy of needs, we know that the lower needs operate by deficiency and are powerfully driven until gratified. The higher needs operate in a different way. As Maslow said, it is a motivational life of ongoing actualization of potentials, capacities, and talents. Higher needs are less dependent on the environment and less dominated by adverse external circumstances with the innate and restless drive to fulfill our innate desire to be all we can be.

Our thoughts and the intentional meanings we create govern how we experience the world. The very acts of being and becoming should not be considered contradictory or mutually exclusive. Either approaching or arriving are both in themselves rewarding. As Maslow wrote, *"Heaven lies waiting for us through life."*

Clearly, all of this occurs through relationships. Communicating and relating are central facets to leading a meaningful and purposeful life. This process requires power of choice and will to take responsibility and ownership of our perceptions and responses to the environment.

We surely have an instinctoid nature due our genetic encoding, but it is our thoughts that create our destinies, not our DNA encoding into our genes. We need to embrace challenges and ambiguity with creativity and escape from the man-made chains of stereotypes and biases built and propagated by the social set.

As simple as it is, we all move away from pain and seek pleasure, but the key lies in the meaning we attach to things and to all the frames that govern the whole process of perception—the deep connection between the real world and our minds.

SEARCHING MEANING

What the experience means to us conditions the experience itself.

By quoting Nietzsche's "*He who has a why to live for can bear with almost any how*" as a could-be guiding motto for all psychotherapeutic and psycho-hygienic efforts regarding prisoners, Viktor Frankl wrote, "*One should not search for an abstract meaning of life. Everyone has his own specific vocation or mission in life to carry out a concrete assignment which demands fulfillment.*" He considered what he defined as "Super Meaning" as the ultimate meaning necessarily exceeding and surpassing the finite intellectual capacities of men. To this regard, he developed logotherapy (*logos* meaning deeper than logic) focusing on the will to meaning as the worth of life, which is based on the premise that human beings' primary motivational force is to find meaning in life, which is opposed to existence being driven by power or pleasure, as proposed by Adler and Freud. Meaning added to intention equals intentional meaning and influences our realities. We construct the reason for which we want or desire something. From meaning, we give birth to everything we deem valuable. At a physical level, we surely have innate survival drives, but at a psycho-level, it is all about meaning.

Cybernetics, for instance, is a broad field of study of the structure of regulatory systems, most applicable to language-based systems where action by the system causes some change in its environment and that change is fed to the system via a feedback process that causes the system to adapt to new conditions, changing and affecting behavior via a "circular causal" relationship. It is a self-reflexive process that feeds back onto itself. Our brains do the very same thing as cybernetic systems. We feed back on our own thoughts, and we build our meanings and new thoughts— new information. This is the core and most important aspect of our lives, and it is considered the main drive of all our actions.

We start by linking and associating things. We then process external stimuli by linking things to our internal references as a Pavlovian capacity to reflect back on our feelings and thoughts and choose the better way to respond. This stimulus-response mechanism undergoes feedback information processing and results back into our behavior.

As Neuro-Semantics teaches, the basic formula is E-B = I-S (External Behavior = Internal States).

Everything pops out from the worlds of meanings we have created.

STRANGE DAYS

Strange Days is a 1995 cyberpunk science fiction film starring Ralph Fiennes and the gorgeous Juliette Lewis. In 1999 during the last days of the old millennium,

Los Angeles became a dangerously volatile zone of violent crimes. Former cop Lenny Nero turned into a street-hustler dealing with SQUID data discs containing recorded memories and emotions. The Superconducting Quantum Interference Device (SQUID) records events directly from the wearer's cerebral cortex and, when played back through minidisc devices, it allows the user to experience the recorder's memory as if it was his own experience.

Adapted to the movie for other purposes, SQUID is no fantasy. It is a very sensitive magnetometer used to measure the strength or direction of a magnetic field that operates via the Josephson Effect, a phenomenon of current that flows indefinitely long without any voltage applied across two superconductivity devices coupled by a weak link.

The interesting fact here is people being willing to buy others' emotions and memories. Paradoxically, many people are not satisfied with their lives and wish to be in someone else's shoes. It might be because of belongings, of studies, achievements, fortune, and fame—pretty much everything you can think of with regard to the meanings they have created. Others spend their time dreaming and never take any action to actualize their wishful thinking. Most of the time people who are not happy with themselves become victims of their own lives. They see the world with the victim's glasses and do their very best to blame others for their misfortune and poor existing conditions. Meanings are powerful.

The good news is that we do not need a SQUID device to live happy memories and make our dreams real. It depends on our states of mind and the quality of the realities we re-present or imagine inside our heads when building up meanings over meanings.

STATES OF MIND

We do not need to possess a SQUID device to be the architects of our future; it is our meanings explanations, and interpretations of the world that make us emotional. First of all, we shall learn to master our own states, think strategically about where we want to go, and make our dreams meaningful and passionate by creating a compelling vision of our future. States are meanings, attitudes, moods, and emotions that occur in our holistic mind-body system.

A state is a dynamic and ever-changing energy field that is always in flux.

Neuro-Semantic Meta States are states about states, a state of consciousness (mental or emotional) that is above or beyond another state and which is about that other state of awareness. The Meta (above) state begins with the thoughts of emotion of a primary state. It is a dynamic complex of the entire mind-body-emotion system. All our experiences begin with a primary state, which is representation-driven by sights, sounds, and sensations.

All begins with a state as a combination of thinking, emoting, and physiological experience—in other words, mind, emotion, and body. Then, we move up to a more complex structure made of the same stuff that makes up our primary states. These higher states are primarily informed and driven by linguistics. Michael L. Hall argues, *"At the Meta levels our higher states involve beliefs, understandings, values, interpretations, evaluations, judgments,...These conceptual experiences, as Meta States, involve abstract understanding which require language. And while we can sometimes do this with single words, it usually requires sentences involving more complex linguistic structures. This takes us up to the level of beliefs, understandings, paradigms, etc. Understandings that we develop about principles, laws, processes, causation, etc. And, of course, this is the domain of the Meta Model about how language works as you construct your model of the world.*" It might be that we have constructed an ill reality full of toxic beliefs, and we need to break it down, challenge, and explore the very semantic structure of our thoughts to take junk off our conceptual constructs.

Everything begins with a neutral state, which is neither good nor evil. To experience a state of mind and emotion we must perceive some kind of stimuli. If we believe or perceive that everything is negative, we will perceive everything in a negative way, through negative lenses, and attract negative things to support this way of thinking. Toxic and venomous states might habituate and become normalcy, but there is absolutely no obligation to be in a default state. There is always a choice.

States of mind influence what we think or display behaviorally. Just changing how we perceive things might leverage and shift our states or behaviors. Sometimes, a smile has the power to change moods and alter people's states of mind. On the other hand, we will not be able to manage other people's states of mind until we're able to manage our own.

What about telling your partner that he/she is beautiful and the best thing that ever happened to you? What about telling your colleague that you will do all the work for him/her? What about telling your parents how much you appreciate and love them?

What about creating meaning for your publics?

SINGULARITY

Dr. Aubrey de Grey is a biomedical gerontologist based in Cambridge, UK, and he is the Chief Science Officer of SENS Foundation, a California-based charity dedicated to combating the aging process. SENS is an acronym for "Strategies for Engineered Negligible Senescence". It is best defined as an integrated set of medical techniques designed to restore youthful molecular and cellular structure to aged tissues and organs. Essentially, this involves the application of regenerative medicine to the problem of age.

De Grey believes on stretching out our lifespan in the quest for immortality and to keep our bodies physically youthful by fighting the aging process. In an interview, he said that we absolutely need a good biological housekeeping, taking trash out of our cells, seeing that inevitably some garbage gets in. Hence, we would need to free our bodies from these build ups. He is convinced that he will find bacteria that are able to break down the substances that accumulate junk into our bodies by introducing these enzymes into our cells to stop the aging process.

We need to get rid of junk and build up strong quality meanings.

GET RID OF JUNK

DNA stands for Deoxyribonucleic Acid.

This nucleic acid is believed to contain the genetic instructions used in the development and functioning of all known living organisms. For many years, scientists have been studying the DNA structure and gave birth to the strong belief that genes rule our lives.

English naturalist Charles R. Darwin established that all species descended from a common ancestry and put forward the scientific argument for the Theory of Evolution by means of natural selection. According to the modern Neo-Darwinian evolutionary synthesis, we might infer that our evolved brain has only two distinct objectives in mind:

survival and competition—a modern law of the jungle made real by many theoreticians. This reminds me of Sigmund Freud, who was obsessed with sex and believed that, over a life time, we just want sex (I know that you are thinking he was right). However, DNA and genes do not govern our lives.

Developmental biologist Bruce Lipton argues that DNA does not control our lives and that the life of a cell is governed by its physical and energetic environment, not by its genes (which are programs used to build cells, tissues, and organs). Eukaryotic cells with a nucleus are organisms whose cells contain complex structures enclosed within membranes and possess the same functional properties we have (e.g. nervous system, digestive system, reproductive system). Lipton studied what most scientists on a global level did not even take into account from a brand new perspective that was considered (and still is) heretic. He redefined the importance of the cell (mainly its membrane and not the nucleus), finding similarities in definition to a computer chip. This is a perfect twist that overturns biology's teachings and supports the fact that thoughts govern our lives, not our DNA.

Lipton views organisms as a community of cells. Our perception is the awareness of the external environment, and our holistic mind-body system is made up by cells. Our cells are clever and have learned to differentiate themselves into a community. Our nervous system, the brain being the biggest organ, coordinates and commands the behavior of all the other organs.

With its structure of neurons and axons, neuro-impulse transmitters and receptors work to abstract patterns of neuro-impulses and energy.

At this stage we are back into the mind, brain, and body dilemma. Aristotle spoke for the unity of mind, whereas, later on, others argued that natural living wholes are like machines or the doctrine of dualism—the coexistence between a nonphysical substance, the mind, and body. Mind and body are a dynamic process. There is plenty of evidence that we are semantic creatures and that we possess a powerful self-reflexive consciousness. We have the power to think and emote over our thinking and feelings. We have the power of choice.

We shall not be victims of the false belief that we cannot change our lives at our will. Beliefs govern our lives, and beliefs are thoughts that we have validated with the help of our self-reflexive consciousness. Seeing that our brain feeds on everything with no particular distinction, it is extremely vital to give it quality food to lead a healthy life.

The matter of our lives is not DNA; it is how we map the territory. It is our mapping that creates reality. Surely, we are conditioned by old habits and by other social, individual, cultural, and even neurological constraints, but, if some of those do not serve us well, we need to change strategy and optimize our thinking. Our mind produces thoughts and our neurological system processes them by feeding back onto itself. We need meaningful and quality information for our brains. We need to be very selective to be in sync with ourselves.

We need to get rid of sabotaging meanings.

EMOTIONAL ABILITY

Ability is the capacity to perform some task. A person's overall ability contains two distinct sets of factors: *intellectual* and *physical abilities.* Physical ability relates to the capacity to perform tasks demanding power, stamina, strength, and characteristics alike, whereas intellectual ability might be defined in various ways with regard to our mental processes.

Intelligence Quotient (IQ) is often cited as a method for assessing a person's intelligence on the basis of several standardized tests; whereas the Emotional Intelligence (EI) is more concerned with the set of mental abilities related to emotions and the processing of emotional information that contribute to logical thought and intelligence, in general. The frequently mentioned dimensions of the standardized tests are usually *number aptitude, verbal comprehension, perceptual speed, inductive and deductive reasoning, spatial visualization, and memory*. Multiple intelligence, on the other hand, considers a broader range of subparts (cognitive, social, emotional, and cultural).

Many believe that results are a prediction of good or bad performance, a mirror of either job and life fit and how you cope with any challenge. These standardized tests are often used by HR departments and are widely taught in universities at bachelor and master degree levels worldwide to adjust stereotypes to people, and vice versa, for them to adapt to the system and the environment as expected by the social set.

These tests might give cues on how the person is, but their validity shall be questioned seeing that, eventually, a "psycho-logical test" cannot stand a comparison with real-life, hands-on performance.

Everything can be learned.

LEARNING OCCURS THROUGH OUR ENTIRE LIFE

Research spans from Pavlov's findings on the stimulus-response classical conditioning to the Operant Conditioning theory by Harvard Professor B.F. Skinner, who argued that behavior is a function of its consequences on a reinforcement/punishment basis, to social learning by observing other people or being told about something.

We are a needy species and we are innately curious through the developmental stages of our lives. We are born with a predisposition to learn, and it is argued that each of us can learn to perform any task. As obvious as it might be, we can all learn to play tennis, but we probably won't beat Swiss champ Roger Federer. The same goes for everything else, from sports to classical music and so on. As psychiatrist Thomas Stephen Szasz said, *"Knowledge is gained by learning; trust by doubt; skill by practice; and love by love."*

Maslow discovered and suggested that we all go through a four-step process in order to gain competency and mastery:

1. **Unconscious Incompetence:** We do not even know that we are ignorant about something.
2. **Conscious Incompetence:** We become aware that we do not know a thing about something.
3. **Conscious Competence:** We are learning and we become effective in that something.
4. **Unconscious Competence:** The unconscious controls our bodily functions, stored memories, wisdom, creativity, and other mental habits.

Whenever we learn something, it becomes automated. And we are no longer aware of how we do it. We master it and perform it naturally—we become unconsciously competent at it. The funny thing is that we then have difficulties in teaching others how we do that something. If asked to, we'd need to go through a fifth step, rediscovering the "how-to."

It is also worth noting that we learn best quickly, and information gets its own neuronal pathways in the brain. For the time being, we have the wonderful opportunity to program ourselves as no other machine can do—yet. Speed plus repetition equal learning, and the impossible becomes possible with the right attitude and mental strategy modeling. Practice and repetition help to integrate and reinforce newly acquired skills into the mind-body holistic system. Anyone can attain personal excellence. It just takes two things: discipline to stretch the boundaries plus ongoing learning to further develop and prioritize what is truly meaningful.

"Start by doing what's necessary; then do what's possible; and suddenly you are doing the impossible."

(SAN FRANCIS OF ASSISI)

THE KNIFE GRINDER

Human beings learned to sharpen their tools well before steel and iron came along. Later on, grinding, or sharpening knives, became a job performed by a man cycling around towns. This job is no longer needed, seeing that we find it much easier to resort to technology or throw away our knives when dull.

We cannot do the same when it comes to sharpening our skills. Statistics and research demonstrate that people hate to read, investigate, and learn new things. This is a pity seeing that ongoing learning leads to a more optimistic view of life, plus being charming and more knowledgeable in social and business settings.

Alfred Korzybski emphasized that we live in a process world of continual change; whereas Maslow, in his holistic view of human nature, said that life is a continual series of choices by demonstrating the pressure of men to fulfill an innate desire and pressure toward growth and self-development. The process world we live in is constantly and ceaselessly changing and ongoing changing requires either ongoing development and refreshing our vision, our goals, and our skills to adapt and to cope with these requirements.

Some say that knowledge is power. Knowledge is a powerful tool. Being a social species, our lives are made up of interpersonal relationships and business is done with and through people. We need to be knowledgeable. We need to be well-informed in both business and our private lives.

This does not mean that we must be enrolled in every possible academic course and be engaged in higher education programs throughout our entire lives. It means that we must possess a fluid mind and the necessary curiosity to keep learning new meanings. Learning shall never stop in our entire lifespan. We should never stop growing. We should never stop being curious. We should never stop chasing our dreams, and we must possess an ongoing learning attitude.

In *The 7 Habits of Highly Effective People*, Stephen Covey tells of a woodman who was having a hard time sawing a tree. The reason? He was so busy sawing that he did not have time... to sharpen the saw.

Sharpening your skills must be (or become) a habit of yours. Exercise and practice until you are able to do things effortlessly. Then keep practicing and make *Kaizen* (Japanese for "continuous improvement") your way of life.

THE MATRIX

The Matrix is a 1999 sci-fi movie. The movie depicts a future in which human perception of reality is simulated by machines to subdue the human population and use their brains as sources of energy. The film contains tons of references to hacker and cyberpunk subcultures, encompassing several areas of interest, from philosophy to religion and from fiction to Japanese animation.

Neo, a computer programmer who is also a hacker, feels that something is wrong with the fictional reality he lives in and seeks answers with regard to the meaning of cryptic references on his computer—the Matrix. He is driven to Morpheus, who offers him a choice: taking a blue pill would allow him to continue his life as usual, whereas taking the red one would allow him to learn the truth about the Matrix. Neo chose the latter and discovered that the year they were living in was 2199 in a world of despair and war between humans and intelligent machines. Not in 1999.

We create our meanings and we are driven by meaning. We create our own unique Matrix.

The Neuro-Semantic Matrix model is a systemic model about human framing, style of thinking, and meaning-making. Reminiscent of the Semantic Web Layer Cake, we live in a mind-body Matrix of complex layers made up of beliefs, thoughts, values, ontologies, and meaning.

What others learned and encoded through centuries in a symbolic form allowed who came later to begin where the former generation left off. This model offers a giant contribution to our understanding of our model of the world and how we invent and create meaning.

THE NEURO-SEMANTIC MATRIX MODEL

The Matrix Model begins with a simple mind-body state of awareness. It begins responding to some event or stimuli in the world. We then re-present things in our minds. We associate, label, evaluate, abstract, summarize, and frame between levels of awareness, and we give meanings to things, holding them for future reference. By mapping our internal reference structures, we create belief frames about any given domain or abstract concept. Our meanings and beliefs are commands to our neurological system.

Our mind-body-emotion system works as a holistic and dynamic system where multiple things fire off simultaneously. Our neuro-semantic system allows multiple feedback loops and does not work in a typical Aristotelian-linear fashion. As Neo, our Matrix awareness begins when we understand how we re-present information to ourselves and how we create our worlds of meanings, psychic movies, and mental maps of the world.

Simplistically, information goes in, we process it internally by constructing our reality of the world, and we output energy (feelings, nervous system responses, emotions, speech, behavior), making use of the feedback of our action. It's absolutely not static. We create and solidify our layers through education, culture, learning, modeling, repetition, and so on.

Our Matrix is a network of beliefs and cumulative learning from many experiences, and each one of us operates from a very different Matrix. As the complex Semantic Web Layer Cake, we may find layers upon layers of greater complexity in the human being. On the other hand, we are—for the time being—the most complex machine on the planet.

The Matrix Model is made of content matrices (Self, Power, Time, People, and World) and process matrices (State, Meaning, and Intention). The content matrices give a person's ideas and frames of reference meaning that gives form and significance to experiences, whereas the process matrices give the form and structure of personality and experience regardless of the person or content.

Matrices are interrelated and influence each other.

Each one of us lives in a totally unique Matrix.

THE SELF

"And remember, no matter where you go, there you are," Confucius said.

There are many facets of our self-concept that influence our thoughts and feelings. Modern psychology defines it as the cognitive and affective representation of our identity. This process starts from the very beginning of our lives when we are named. We start by learning things, such as *I am Francesco, it is Mine, it is Me,* and become self-conscious and self-aware.

Since then, we keep growing and developing our sense of self, creating multiple meanings in terms of self-esteem, self-efficacy, social-self, business-self, self-reliance, self-confidence, relational-self, and so on. We all possess many "ourselves" and it all depends on the meanings we have attributed to ourselves in our reality of the world, in our Matrix.

Am I worthy? Am I not? Confidence in yourself is how you talk to yourself. Most people do not have a high self-esteem; many are not even able to separate their behaviors from their selves and end up personalizing everything that happens to them. A top manager might rely on his status to define his self, while others who haven't been so successful in their working life might believe that they are not worth a dime.

Personalizing is a major problem.

What about you? What meanings have you attributed to your selves?

Do you like your many selves and feel valuable and worthy as a human being, or are you needy to prove something to others in order to feel respectable?

WHO'S GOT THE POWER?

Is power in the hands of the governors or the governed? The élite or the masses?

It really depends.

In the Feudal era, brute force was used as a control mechanism. Then, strategies to mold public opinion became indirect and shifted from the hands of the monarchy to subtle techniques of controlling attitudes and thoughts through PRopaganda, leading to consumerism and artificial values creation instead of authentic and robust meanings.

Power is all about resourcefulness and efficacy in response. It is the ability to intentionally mold behaviors, opinions, and attitudes.

It is our sense of power. Throughout ages, warriors, governments, politicians, seducers, you, and I have all desired to have more power. Courts, tribes, communities, and civilization itself have always formed around people with power, such as kings, emperors, and other great leaders.

To date, coercion left place to covert tactics and subtle moves because warfare deception and tactical thinking might lead to suspicion. As such, they are not welcomed into our society and might lead to counter moves from envious people. Let's imagine a typical office setting. You are working hard, you are good at what you are doing, and you bring results in. The lights are on you. You end up fired.

This happens all the time. It might be that you have outshined or clouded your boss' radiance. You need to understand that there will always be people ready to stab you in the back when your guard is off. As a consequence, you need to learn to adopt the plasticity of a theater actor—royal in your own fashion but, at the same time, extremely careful when it comes to power.

Power comes first from being responsible for our thoughts, feelings, actions, and speech. It comes from being proactive and assertive, not reactive, to events. It comes from careful planning and clear direction in mind.

Be confident but careful of other people. Avoid personalizing events or behaviors. Take control over your life, and avoid traps on your "Parkour." Some people are out there trying to get you. Envy is a nasty beast. Your sense of duty, option, and choice will result in them being unable to ambush you.

Influence is power.

TICK TOCK

Adapted from the 1985 novel by English author Herbert George Wells, *The Time Machine* became a 2002 American sci-fi movie.

It narrates a young nineteenth century inventor who devoted himself to building a time machine, hoping to alter the events of the past. Being unable to alter history back in time, he travels far into the future, where he finds human civilization reverted into a primitive lifestyle.

Time has always been the fount of fascination and has been a major subject for many, from science to philosophy, and it is defined as being part of a measuring system used to sequence events—a conceptual definition of the reality we live in. Time is subjective and it is the same for all of us. However, it all depends on our personal perception of this process. To quote actor Jeremy Irons: "*We all have our time machines. Some take us back, they're called memories. Some take us forward, they're called dreams.*" We all navigate through life representing and encoding time in different ways, depending on our "Time Line."

It is argued that there are two particular representations of time. One is having the past behind us, the future in front, and the present inside ourselves, known as *in time*. Whereas, in the case where the present is in front of you, the future is on the right side, and the past on the left, this is referred to as *through time*.

There is a great difference about how we think, encode, and approach time. The following is our understanding of events and how we map our ideas and concepts of time:

- PAST: Some people live in the past and rely on it for every decision they make.
- PRESENT: Others live in the present. In the "now," for the pleasure of the moment.
- FUTURE: Some find themselves being detached from either past and present issues.

We all have twenty-four hours a day, and we have the power of choosing how to spend every second of those hours. How we think about time and perceive it governs how we feel about something. Once you understand these mental filters, you can look at the past, the present, and the future in many different ways. Undoubtedly, we visualize things in our minds. We create images. Hence, we have the power of altering time. We can anticipate any outcome, either for ourselves or with regard to our publics by creating images.

We can vividly picture ourselves achieving the desired goal or altering our publics' perception, having them seeing themselves in the future, the past, or the present. We are used to giving precedence to a misconception of time. The meanings we map about time greatly influence our lives. By distinguishing and altering the conception of time, we are able to change perspectives. We need to focus on the present and keep an eye at the future without worrying too much about past events, seeing that we cannot alter them but only gain some useful insights.

Time management enables us to control the sequence of events in life, and the ability to use and manage time in an efficient way is not only a competitive advantage.

It is a way of living.

IMAGINARY STRESS MANAGEMENT

Wake Up! Hurry Up! Move! The clock is ticking! No time left! Deadline is yesterday! Right now!

Does this sound stressful? Some say that there are either pros or cons to stressful psychological pressure. Personally, I do not agree with this statement because psychological pressure and stress are not to be considered as synonymous. Stress does not have any positive attribute. In this real-time world, sickened by financial downturns and weakened economic scenarios, it is far too easy (and common) to cry out for being "stressed." How many times have you heard people saying they feel under pressure and stressed out?

What does stress really mean? The American Institute of Stress (AIS) says, "*Stress is difficult for scientists to define because it is a subjective sensation associated with varied symptoms that differ for each of us.*" This is the point. It is a subjective sensation—a subjective experience. It usually involves external factors thrown at us, and if we are overdependent on the external environment, we succumb and surrender. It also depends on the meaning we attach to these events. The funny thing is that meaning does not really exist. We create it. It is a consequence of how we conceptualize the world and represent it in our minds.

At this stage, we can easily infer that stress does not exist in reality. As beauty, it lies in the eye of the beholder. By de-stressing ourselves, we would lead more effective, efficient, and productive lives. Otherwise, our problem-solving skills, creativity, well-being, and so on would be drastically reduced.

<u>The unreal disease and its neuro-semantic cure:</u>

- Recognize the presence of stress symptoms and keep refining your counterstrategies.
- Become more skilled in problem-solving and managing your time.
- Re-frame meanings. Look at the world with another perspective and/or multiple perspectives.
- Avoid extreme cultural relativism, such as the Marxist psychology, etc.
- Relax and calm down. Enjoy life, your passions, and your job.
- Refine your skills in terms of assertiveness.
- Refuse to let external factors manage your life. You are in charge. It is your response-ability.
- Stressed? It is just desserts spelled backwards.

It is absolutely counterproductive to lead a busy but ineffective life. The key lies in working smarter, not harder. Use the time at your disposal in the most efficient way.

"In times of stress, be bold and valiant."

(HORACE)

A MATTER OF PERSPECTIVE

Self-esteem is a term used in psychology to reflect the individual appraisal of one's own worth. Semantically, as the term says, it is the esteem we have of our self. People who value themselves highly turn out to be attractive because of our innate needs to be social and to be a part of groups and our attraction to value. People with low self-esteem provoke opposite feelings.

Self-esteem differs from self-confidence. The first is the way you feel about yourself. The latter is the way you feel about your skills and abilities. Social psychologists argue that, in order to develop self-esteem, you need to dedicate time to do whatever makes you feel good.

Dedicate time to your passions. It helps to be proud of who you are and the way you are living your life. Confidence in one's abilities and skills is not that easy. It involves lots of practice, repetition, patience, and effort.

To this regard, it is extremely important to have a vision—to have dreams. The ongoing development of our skills and competencies is at the heart of our growth and overall development. This involves ego-strength, seeing that we all feel a bit confused, stressed, and foggy when faced with new challenges. If we spend our time dreaming, we'll never go forward, whereas when we become skilled at doing something, boredom kicks in. There should be a balance between being afraid of the new and becoming bored of performing some sort of task. Skills and competences are built through challenges. Challenges allow us to be able to face life and to get better at facing new challenges. Try, experience, and put effort into your passions and dreams. Face your fears by not being afraid to do so.

Being afraid is a typical characteristic of people who lack self-confidence. They tend to exaggerate about things to impress others, they try hard to get attention, they always want to be right, they want approval, and they are often aggressive.

Most people prefer to live in their comfort zones. They never stretch the boundaries of life. They hate change.

They are afraid of standing up and expressing their point of view.

They are fearful—fearful of doing it wrong, of failure, of rejection, of disappointment. As Theodore Roosevelt said, *"The only man who makes no mistakes is the man who never does anything."* Mistakes happen all the time and provide a great opportunity to learn. Consider any mistake as feedback to get better at what you are doing (and not to repeat that mistake). Independently of your learned stereotypes and meanings, you will see the world differently.

As cognitive theories teach, our moods are created by cognition and thoughts. How you look at things and the meaning you attribute to them can make a very big difference.

It is simply a matter of perspective.

"The only real failure in life is the failure to try."

(SVEN-GÖRAN ERIKSSON)

HOW MUCH DO YOU ESTEEM YOUR MANY SELVES?

Self-esteem is a barometer for self-confidence. We all desire and deserve to be respected and accepted by others. We all love a sincere compliment, and we're even quite good at easily spotting unnecessary and insincere flattery.

On the other hand, most people on earth do not hold a high self-esteem and a solid sense of unconditional value. Many feel they're never good enough at what they do, not popular, and not nice looking.

When it comes to assessing ourselves, we are the worst judges and often express no pity. That is the main reason for which trust and recognition leverage people's morale with no weight on your balance sheet. It costs nothing.

The way you talk to others, including the substance of your message, influences minds. The way you talk to your selves is by no means less important. With our sense of competence, effectiveness, and ability to live up to our values, we can change our attitudes. As Martin Seligman wrote, "*Both learned helplessness and learned optimism are ways of thinking about the amount of power or influence we exert in the world.*" Each describes how we frame our realities and how we engage with others.

And ourselves.

OVER THE EDGE

Enthusiasm is important. Fight for your dreams and stop making up silly excuses to procrastinate.

Self-respect is a primal characteristic to living well. Yet, overconfidence is not a good trait, and you'd not be considered as such, seeing that supremely confident people do not really exist in reality apart from a façade.

Be competent. Be confident. Avoid personalizing. Yet, at the same time be humble.

DOORS OF PERCEPTION

Perception is a process. We try to interpret and organize information via our representation systems to attain understanding and give meaning to the surrounding environment. We know that the map is not the territory, and perceptions can be substantially different from reality itself.

Our perceptions are influenced by a plurality of factors, such as expectations, interests, experience, and attitudes, at the core of our intimate individual level and the situational factors as either the context and the characteristics of the target of our attention. The difference in perceptions is imposed by different filtering processes, stereotypes, and sets of constructed meanings.

So, what are the main reasons for which people behave in a certain way? What are underlying motives causing different perceptions? In social psychology, the Attribution theory was first proposed by Austrian psychologist Fritz Heider and further developed by others to understand how individuals explain causes of behavior and events. The first thing to be said is that the inferences we make up vary depending on the target. We are keen to judge people differently from other (inanimate) objects because we usually try to explain behavior. We also draw a distinction between issues that are believed to be under one's personal control (internal) and, vice versa, the result of outside sources (external).

For example, it's Monday morning. You call your boss and inform that you're going to miss the day because you do not feel well. This might be perceived as something under your control. On the contrary, if it's Monday morning and you call the office to inform you'll be late because the city traffic is paralyzed by bad weather conditions, that might be perceived as an external factor—something that is not under your control.

In addition, there are three subgroups that act as leverage to the previous distinctions:

- Distinctiveness: Is this your unusual? If you've never missed a Monday, you might get away with it. If it is the norm, it is your fault.
- Consensus: How many people are experiencing the same situation (being not well or having problems because of the bad weather conditions)? If you are the only one, it is your fault.
- Consistency: Is missing a day or being late is a common behavior of yours? Again, if it is, it is your fault.

We have the tendency to overvalue internal factors and underestimate the external ones when judging others. We are quick to jump to conclusions and to blame others. At the same time, we have a strong tendency to attribute our own successes to internal factors, while putting the blame to external ones for our failures. Just imagine that yesterday you went to the stadium to see your favorite football team.

- Scenario 1: The team wins! (Most likely you are going to say: <u>We Won</u>!)
- Scenario 2: The match is lost! (Most likely you are going to say: Losers! <u>They lost</u> the game!)

In life, we are so used to filtering things that we do not even know the reason for it. Fact is that we selectively interpret the world on the basis of the meanings we have constructed. Having limited capacity for processing information, we rely on these mental filters to avoid information overload.

We may draw a general impression about others on the basis of a single characteristic as long versus short hair (Halo effect), we tend to paragon individuals and our perceptions of others often based on how we've been influenced by other people we have recently encountered (Contrast effect), we might attribute our own characteristics to others (Projection), and we are very good at judging people on the basis of the group to which they belong (Stereotyping).

Perception is how we interpret the world through our re-presentational system. What meanings do we attach to events? What are the meanings we have constructed with regard to some experience, concept, or idea? Do we have a predisposition to perceive things in a certain way and the tendency to justify our decisions, even if proven wrong?

"If the doors of perception were cleansed, everything would appear as it is: infinite."

(WILLIAM BLAKE)

PEOPLE ARE STRANGE

We construct our mental maps and beliefs about everything. Although we all live on earth, we live in many different and unique worlds—our unique minds. The common thing is that our behavior is often influenced by the rules imposed on us by the social set and learned habits. Other times, we are the ones to decide.

How we relate to others is part of our emotional intelligence and social skills. Our understanding of the world, of our culture, of the society we live in, and the rules are very important. Fundamentally, we have our general philosophies about everything, from politics to football games and from school to business.

Are the frames of meaning you built up serving you well in the worlds you live in?

"The most important single ingredient in the formula of success is knowing how to get along with people."

(T. ROOSEVELT)

YOU LIKE PEOPLE WHO ARE JUST LIKE YOU

Don't you?

Just think of the friends you like. What do they mean to you? What is so special about them? It's a human characteristic. We love to be part of something. We like people who have the same interests, tastes, beliefs, values, status, et cetera—people who are, in some way, similar to us.

Appearance, trustworthiness, charisma, character, credibility, and reputation are effective means of influence and persuasion to leverage biases and heuristics and largely determine cognitive reactions.

Likable.

BE LIKABLE

Do women really evaluate resources as power and status (or the potential to develop such) to a higher degree than men, who are more driven by physical appearance and sex?

Some say so because, as individuals, we are ego-centric and egoistical. Emotion beats cynical logic most of the time. So, what is the simplest trick to be liked by others? We all like the spotlight to be on ourselves. We love to tell our stories. We love other people to listen and to pay attention to what we have to say. As a consequence, focusing on others will result in being liked. People love to talk about their interests, their families, their values, and their lives. If you ever keep talking about yourself, you will end up boring your audience, and if you fall for religion and politics with people who do not share your views, you will probably get into big trouble.

Listening is key. By listening you allow the other person to tell his or her story. Good listeners are always appreciated. In addition, you gather intel about what other people's interests are, what they deem meaningful, and how they know what/that they think they know. You learn more about them by making them feel good about themselves around you.

This is no fake communication. It'd be better for you to truly care and be kind in every setting. Being interested in others' lives is a central facet of social psychology and the influence process. By being a good listener and helping people out, you will be associated with good feelings.

Your main objective is to make others feel good around you. By being charming, you will project a positive attitude and radiate warmth.

Everyone needs to feel appreciated and loved.

Like attracts like.

WHY IS INFLUENCE IMPORTANT?

Most of the time, the source of the message is you. Being able to influence is a very important skill. It is a form of social influence, a process that occurs when you affect other people's behaviors, emotions, ideas, attitudes, and actions.

Seeing that human beings cannot not communicate, it is impossible not to influence or persuade others. It would be a paradox.

Over time, the term *manipulation* gained a negative connotation, as for PRopaganda. It evokes brainwashing techniques as in film *The Manchurian Candidate* (1959) where the son of an American political family is brainwashed into becoming a Communist Party assassin. This is because that many silly compliance professionals have sabotaged the win/win formula for their profitable and personal interests. Influencing other people at their disadvantage does not work in the long run, and, in today's business world, short-term compliance is neither tempting nor desirable if compared to long-term fruitful relationships. The ultimate goal should be that everyone benefits and everyone's happy. Understanding human nature, people's mindsets and decision making processes, and mastering communication are fundamental aspects of everyday life.

Likability determines success. Opinions and impressions create meanings that stick.

MAGIC MIRROR OF THE WALL, WHO IS THE FAIREST OF THEM ALL?

Many people do believe that life is not fair.

What does appearance mean to you? The majority of us are not even close to looking as gorgeous as Daphne Groeneveld, Emmy Rossum, Julia Roberts, Brad Pitt, George Clooney, Keanu Reeves, Camille Rowe, Georgia Frost, Wesley Snipes, or Ashley Judd. Many are not happy with their looks or, at least, not satisfied as they wish.

To a certain degree, the fact that life is not fair is true.

Looks matter a lot and may even intoxicate our minds with self-sabotaging, venomous thoughts. Tons of research shows that people tend to associate traits of intelligence, kindness, and trust with people who are attractive. These people are considered more talented, more friendly, and happier than others. It may not be fair, but it's how things are. It is not important to be; it is absolutely essential to appear.

Attractiveness really makes a difference. Appearance and mannerism are not to be undervalued in the social sets we live in. If you are perceived as attractive and sexy, you will surely make a better impression and gain compliance with the people you deal with.

Before meeting anyone, what you see/hear/feel largely determines the follow-up course of action. It provides you with either a positive or negative input. It is an invisible force creating meanings and pushing you to know, or not to know, that person. The good news is that anyone can do something to enhance features and be attractive. Clothes and jewelry are fruits of the consumerist society we live in. Wearing Armani or Gucci all the time tells your status, but this way to improve one's looks can be quite lavish. The key lies in looking appropriate and in your best shape in every setting. As we know, the context is as important as the source the message. Mannerism includes education as well. Some are not educated and others do not care and miss out on self-care. Personal hygiene is a starting point.

Taking care of your skin, your hair, being neat and tidy, showering every day, not biting your nails, and brushing your teeth and your gums have no substitutes. Unless you are a hygiene psycho, no matter how you think you are doing, I would suggest getting a third party's impression. Your partner and your friends might experience difficulties in telling you that your breath smells like a sewer or your favorite bubble bath was originally produced as a pesticide. Asking for professional (beauty institutes) help is a key factor seeing that we are absolutely not unbiased. The quality of your life depends on your daily self-care (aesthetics, quality of your sleep, habits, and yes, even emotional self-care).

Self-care and social skills are married.

PEOPLE JUDGE THE BOOK...
BY ITS COVER

Is making a great first impression important? You bet. We talk without even speaking. Our appearance and our body language are tremendous sources of information for others to make up their minds about us. Appearance is a matter of life and death. You have just a handful of seconds (between zero and one) to make the first impression.

A glance is quick. A glance wraps it all up. It takes just a glance.

As we are quick to judge others, others are as quick to judge us, either at the professional or personal level. With our appearance, physiology, posture, and body language, we give others a lot of information about ourselves, including our feelings, attitudes, emotions, and lifestyle. People make up their minds and decide, with a *Speedy-Gonzales veloc-ity*, whether to like us, trust us, want to do business with us, go out on a date, or want to have sex with us in an instant.

A snapshot.

A glance.

It might sound cynical, but the first impression is usually based on physical appearance and mannerism. Most of the time, we do not even have the opportunity of a second shot—no possibility to speak out, no possibility for others to know us at a deeper level. They made up their mind in a glance. As a consequence, it is categorically imperative to look appropriate in every setting. You would not wish to find yourself at a cocktail party in your under-wear (*although, some kinky-thinkers might appreciate it*) or playing volleyball at the beach in your cocktail party dress. You would not wish to show up at an important business meeting with top executives as you would to at a pajama party. There is a time and a place for everything. As obvious as it might sound, in case we are to speak, our verbal communication needs to be totally congruent with our body language.

Unless one masters it, body language is not easy to fake.

It all starts with appearance. You might even be surprised to know that physical features, poise, grace, elegance, mannerism, and the like can be enhanced by anyone. Remember that people make decisions based on emotions driven by meanings, not logic, and are quick to glance at you. Most people are more interested in appearance than substance. As a result, the secret keys lie in appearance, mannerism, and emotional states.

The wrong first impression would mean running against a wall and would never lead to being other people's mental landscape architect.

THE SEXIST SIDE OF SOCIETY

A woman in a sweater elicits a different response as the same girl in bikini or who is topless. A shirtless male elicits a different response compared to his suited-up counterpart. Research demonstrates this hedonistic way of thinking.

Dressing for who you want to be is common advice. Dressing appropriate to the setting is just common sense.

THE KEY TO BRANDING: PERCEPTION MANAGEMENT

We identify ourselves with brands. We use their products and services to define our identity. This set of expectations is powerful. Everything determines how much we like something, from the label we wear to the words we use. Our appearance is important.

Recognition, reputation, and familiarity are on the top of the list when it comes to branding. In other words, it is all about your perceptions. Over the history of advertising, it has been clearly demonstrated that blind tests on products show that some labels were much better than others, despite the fact that was not the case on the market. The best example ever is the blind test between Coke and Pepsi, commonly known as the Pepsi challenge. We recognize labels. We associate brand names on a reputation basis. With brands we signal our identity to others. We express our identity.

Association, recognition, and familiarity are extremely important. Priming and implicit memory are as important as recognition, declarative memory, and semantic priming to advertisers.

Perception management is the key. In general, how people interpret things and what these things mean to them largely conditions and determines everything about how they make up their minds about you and, consequently, relate to you.

Business is done by, with, and through people. It is the result of all the interactions between the company and its publics.

ONLINE OPINIONS

People judge the book by its cover. Your physical appearance and mannerisms condition people's perceptions. The same happens with your online presence with the very first thing they see (your picture, the design of your website, your content). What you say comes second. Is your public image in sync with what you want others to think of you? In the virtual world, you are what you publish.

CHARISMA

Napoleon Bonaparte, Winston Churchill, Martin Luther King, Adolf Hitler, Bill Clinton, and others have always been portrayed as possessing charismatic qualities.

A great amount of research found that charismatic people possess an infectious personality. Their personality traits induce others to follow them, to copy their body language, and even to mime their facial expressions.

Documented studies isolated six main characteristics of charismatic leaders:

- They have a vision.
- They are willing to take risks to achieve the vision.
- They motivate with passion.
- They are sensitive to the environmental constraints.
- They are sensitive to followers' needs.
- They display behaviors out of the ordinary.

Charismatic people have optimistic views and passion, and they are considered catalysts for generating enthusiasm and fervor. They are masters of the art of influence and are said to enhance their followers' self-esteem and confidence. As we know, when a number of living beings are gathered together, they place themselves under the magic spell of the charismatic figure. The crowd is not capable of existing without a leader.

As quoted by Le Bon, Maximilien de Robespierre, one of the most influential and controversial figures of the French Revolution, was so enchanted by Jean-Jacques Rousseau's philosophical ideas that he employed inquisition methods to propagate them.

Charismatic thought leaders influence and infect people's minds.

Charisma enchants.

YOU ARE WRONG

The secret of charisma is for people to feel good when around you—being enchanted and drawn to someone like a magnet.

This is vital in any business setting, during presentations, in interpersonal relationships, or even in a romantic conversation. The formula is to know what is meaningful to people and to help them be right, even if they are mistaken. Injecting controversy leads to your interlocutor feeling aversion. Unattractive and negative feelings might then be associated with you.

Here are some rapport-killing sins of unattractive communication:

- Blabbing out irresponsible statements without thinking.
- Constantly taking opposite views.
- Making others feel wrong, uninformed, and silly.
- Interrupting others when they are talking.

- Blaspheming.
- Not listening and not being interested in what others have to say.
- Judging others.
- Complaining and whining all the time.
- Showing self-pity.
- Carrying around negativity and pessimism.
- Insulting.
- Being a know-it-all jerk.
- Gossiping.
- Being meaningless.

One of the keys to effective communication lies in active listening, communicating with our whole bodies, and a mutual disclosure that is respected and welcomed. If you want to be perceived as charismatic and make others feel good when around you, you should do your best to avoid trying to create superiority over others or show low self-esteem by conveying your despair or sadness through the content you share with others via any channel of thought.

"The way we communicate with others and with ourselves ultimately determines the quality of our lives."

(ANTHONY ROBBINS)

THE GOSSIP INNUENDO

Don't you love to gossip sometimes?

People do love gossip. It is very tempting to fall for a gossip innuendo. False allegations and rumors are considered more believable and seductive that the truth. Gossip entertains and gets a lot of attention. People do not bother much in verifying factoids and treat them as true. As a consequence, gossip spreads quickly.

Although it might be socially tempting, gossiping should be avoided because it can undermine your credibility in the eyes of others. Do you like people who are gossiping all the time? No one does. Instead, focus on positive things and bring only nice experiences with you when interacting with people.

Your main duty is to create a nice atmosphere and a nice aura around yourself.

To discredit, to judge and criticize, and to complain all the time are not traits that are very welcomed. If possible, try to avoid this kind of behavior if you do not want to end up alone because everyone avoids you.

CREDIBILITY & EXCELLENCE

Like time, credibility has become a scarce commodity. Credibility does not have anything to do with the good character of the communicator, as Aristotle thought. It is strictly related to people's perceptions, and, as such, it can be manufactured.

Credibility goes arm-in-arm with appearance, reputation, trustworthiness, likability, authority, empathy, and competence as a means to establish a favorable image in the eyes of your audience and to be perceived as you wish. It influences minds. The gossip innuendo and prejudices have the opposite effect.

Flexibility is key and knowledge is a powerful tool at your disposal. Know the anatomy of your audience by gathering intel (market, industry, demographics, hopes, interests, values, dreams, beliefs, culture, traditions), and understand backgrounds, perceptual filters, and the lingo of your publics.

Having done your homework, you may now design, craft, customize, and deliver your charismatic PRopaganda full of meaning to approach your public and orchestrate the circumstances so that you will be perceived as a credible source.

BE KNOWN AS THE AUTHORITY

Bernays wrote, "*The mental equipment of the average individual consists of mass judgments on most of the subjects which touch his daily physical or mental life. These judgments are the tools of his daily being and yet they are his judgments, not only on a basis of research and logical deduction, but for the most part a dogmatic expression accepted on the authority of his parents, his teachers, his church, and his social, his economic and other leaders.*" Authority affects decision-making. As psychology and marketing expert Robert Cialdini argues, "*Information from a recognized authority can provide us a valuable shortcut for deciding how to act in a given situation.*" This is the convenience of automatic obedience.

In decision-making, biases and heuristics always come into play. In business, people are more likely to do business with other people they like, recognize, and trust as credible, authoritative sources.

How can you be recognized as such in your field? To wave master's degrees or PhDs and company awards might be an idea, but what about showing your expertise? Certification does not always equate to authority recognition in people's minds.

To be recognized as such, you must be very knowledgeable—the expert in your field of expertise. How? By leveraging the power of the web and offering well-timed and highly meaningful content to your publics. Before the web came along, businesses ran on huge marketing expenditures to push out their unilateral messages. Now, many still struggle with nomenclature, terminology, and strategies and consider the rise of Internet-related technologies as being new, mysterious ways to connect with consumers directly and engage them in two-way conversation. Long distance text messaging via some signaling technology was invented about 200 years ago—the telegraph. A two-way conversation is no news, but there are literally hundreds of new avenues to reach consumers directly other than the traditional broadcasting, printing, and advertising machinery.

It is much easier to reach a potentially universal audience, but the key still lies in understanding what is really meaningful to people and creating the right circumstances for them to recognize you as the go-to resource.

"The two most powerful warriors are patience and time."

(LEO N. TOLSTOY)

ANTICIPATED LOYALTY

People live in their unique Matrix. They represent the world in a different way than you do. Stereotypes, biases, and shortcuts are the norm. With regard to consumer behavior, your main duty is to thoroughly understand your audience and their real motives and meanings for purchasing your offerings.

Overall, it is quite common for people to repeat past behaviors as a Pavlovian stimulus-response mechanism that is reinforced over time. Just suppose you had a total customer experience at a restaurant—a romantic dinner with your partner, the service was remarkable, the food, the wine…everything was perfect.

The next time you want to experience the same feelings you will go there. We are creatures of habit and we enjoy anticipating the experiences in our minds on the basis of positive past experiences. This is why it is also important to address any concerns by anticipating any negative issue that is likely to come up when propagating your meanings. Any problem might be transformed into opportunity.

This leads to loyalty. Trust and loyalty go arm-in-arm and are not easy to overthrow.

Practice what you preach and never deliver less than promised or expected. People buy from you because they trust you, they like you, and they are loyal to you.

Spring meaningful surprises and exceed on expectations.

PROMISES AND EXPECTATIONS

We're emotional creatures with a tendency to back up everything with logic. No one will ever give you one hundred percent accurate information on the reason for why they did (or do) something, and that's why focus groups and market research questionnaires are a total waste of time and money.

As consumers, we buy experiences.

Few people have no expectations. Expectations might be considered the random variable of the Probability theory, as the maximum-likelihood estimation in statistics, as the predicted measurement of experiments in quantum physics, or, commonly, what's most likely to happen. When you go to your favorite restaurant, you know well in advance what's going to happen. Even before calling to book a table, you know. You anticipate the experience on the basis of your past experiences.

Being emotional creatures of habit, we tend to stick and reinforce our patterned stimulus-response mechanism by repeating pleasant experiences over time. This does not happen when you do not keep your over-advertised promises, and this does not happen when you do not over-deliver on expectations. It does not happen when service is lost through the cracks of profit centers.

Trust and loyalty are non-negotiable commodities.

THE ART OF PERSUASION

Can you say no?

Some people find it extremely difficult. In any case, sometimes all of us comply with some sort of request without even knowing why.

The conventional marketing and sales wisdom teaches that we need to get a prospect to say "yes" several times before closing any sale with a positive answer. We all follow a patterned path in human relations. We perform our scripts as it was a duty, and, as a consequence, there are various patterned manners in which we habitually react to events and triggers in the social set.

The point is that we all love others to comply with our requests. Business is done by, with, and through people, and most of the time we need the cooperation of others to get what we want. Egoistically, we want to get anyone to do anything for us. Compliance professionals know well the boundaries to our decision processes and use persuasive tactics to get us to say "yes" from purchases and votes to donations. These are powerful techniques to influence people's minds and leverage heuristics, biases, and psychological habits, especially if people are not aware that these tactics exist and are mastered by lots of professionals.

Robert Cialdini categorized these weapons of influence around few basic principles. Other experts like Kevin Hogan and Kurt Mortensen developed their models of persuasion and proposed even more laws—all contributing to a better understanding of the reasons for which we say yes.

- Reciprocity: The rule of reciprocity is considered one of the most powerful weapons of psychological persuasion. The rule says, *"We should try to repay, in kind, what another person has provided to us."* It is argued that, if someone does us a favor, we feel obliged to repay the favor in one way or another. This is amplified when the gift is considered valuable and significant, tailored, and even unexpected (it does not have to be expensive).
- Commitment & Consistency: Human beings have an innate desire to appear consistent with what has been done or said in the past. Inconsistency is not seen as a particularly favorite personality trait in today's society. Consistency and commitment are active and public.
- Social Proof: This principle states, *"One means we use to determine what is correct is to find out what other people think is correct and how they behave."* This rule is often applied when we face decisions on how to correctly behave in society.
- Authority: Authority plays a great role of influence in our lives since we are born. Teachers, parents, police, military, and governments all teach us to respect authority, don't they? This clearly affects our decision-making process. We are influenced by those we trust.

- <u>Liking</u>: Liking is activated by uncovering genuine similarities; the "Liking Principle" says that we prefer to comply with the requests of other people we know and like. This rule encompasses the ones above.
- <u>Scarcity</u>: Our decision-making process rapidly changes when we face opportunities that, in a very short time, will be no longer available: "*The idea of potential loss plays a large role in human decision making.*" It is amplified either by comparison or by a sense of loss. Exclusive information, ideas, or limited promotions leverage our interest and attention and facilitate influence.
- <u>Contrast</u>: The Contrast Effect states that subsequent opinions will be viewed in light of previously described opinions. For instance, if the main concern is price, present the most expensive item first. Other items will be seen as less costly and will result in you being able to direct decision-making where you prefer.

Often we do avoid thinking. Thinking requires lots of energy. Faced with infobesity, we do heavily rely on *heuristics and shortcuts* to make sense of all the data we are confronted with each and every day in a *global always-on new reality.*

It's no arcane mystery, our preferences and our decision-making can be easily influenced. We can be easily manipulated at someone else's will by these psychological high-pressure techniques.

What can you do, write, or say to leverage and exploit these natural triggers interchangeably? By knowing and mastering these techniques, one becomes a more effective communicator. On the other side of the coin, it is not always ethical to retaliate using subtle tactics for making profit out of others' rules of thumb and heuristics.

"The most important persuasion tool you have in your entire arsenal is integrity."

(ZIG ZIGLAR)

LIKE SWITZERLAND

The laws of persuasion are neutral.

Like a hammer or a knife, they're not good or bad. It depends on how you use them.

Since antiquity, it has been critical to have the cooperation of other people to get what we want. On the other hand, any process starts within yourself. People are quite good at spotting insincere behavior and flattery. If you are sincere in your intentions and you're perceived as such, you are able to make people comfortable around you by giving out a nice business card yourself—your most personal call-to-action.

The use of coercion, fear, or insincere devilish tricks might get others to comply with your requests as a short-term commitment, but compliance won't last long. The fashionable devil maneuvers never get a long-lasting commitment let alone a win-win relationship.

It is well known that thinking requires lots of cognitive energy, effort, choice, and will. We are overloaded by infobesity, and we do not find the proper time to thoroughly research information. The power of choosing is a burden for many. As a result, we rely on heuristics, biases, and stereotypes.

People are patterned and it is possible to exercise this knowledge to covertly exploit predictable behaviors, which are consistent with one's cognitive life made up of a web of meanings.

Impeccable communication and long-term compliance through cooperation, collaboration, and commitment instead of short-term benefits through intimidation, control, and other coercion tactics should be the aim. If you want to improve the quality of your life, you need to aim for long-term commitment by getting along with others and to use (with integrity) the following psychological laws of persuasion as proposed by leading authority on persuasion and influence Kevin Hogan.

THE LAW OF RECIPROCITY

When someone gives you something of perceived value, you immediately respond with the desire to give something back.

Well before money was accepted as a general means to pay goods and services and/or repay debts, other methods, such as exchanging goods and services with other goods and services, were in place. In the history of informal economic systems, there has always been an exchange of goods, services, and labor.

Some anthropology and sociology researchers define this social behavior as the root of reciprocity. Organizations and compliance professionals have used this tactic by sending us free perfume samples or offering us gadgets, such as pens or other items, knowing that we would often accept the gift with a sense of indebtedness, feeling a compelled desire to give something back. A common example refers to the Hare Krishna when they started to leverage reciprocity by giving people a flower as a gift and having them feel compelled to donate or purchase an edition of the Bhagavad Gita.

Reciprocity causes a sense of obligation—a psychological burden. It is a subconscious trigger. Favors, courtesy, and gifts generate obligations. When others do something for us, we feel obliged to return, in kind, the favor. It is a social conditioning that creates an uncomfortable sense of obligation, which, in turn, drives to alleviate the negative feeling by reciprocating even to people we do not know—to strangers.

As a result the trick is fairly simple: create a need or obligation in the mind of others. Win-win is a core issue and one needs to be interested, engaged, caring, and concerned about others (for real). Advertising or promo pitches are not perceived as such. You need to make promises and keep them by being sublime and giving more than promised. The best business example I could find about how this law is masterfully used in the most positive way is the Inbound Marketing University (IMU). The IMU's Inbound Marketing Certification program is powered by software company HubSpot and it is free of charge. In 2010, HubSpot's Inbound Marketing Manager Rebecca Corliss wrote a blog post explaining the reasons for which this program has no fee.

She explained that, internally, they discussed if they should charge a fee or not to ensure student commitment or to remove the prejudice that *valuable things cannot be free.*" They removed the barrier to entry to good education to provide value to the community, but what's in it for them?

- Reputation (Earning respect from the marketing community and being seen as a helpful resource).
- Give-and-take relationships (More people profiting from the knowledge and tools may need a marketing software program in the future).
- Building unified communities.
- Educating and connecting people.
- Marketing PRopaganda.

Since 2006, when the company was founded, HubSpot experienced exponential growth in terms of customers, revenue, and awards and honors from the business community. Despite the fact that I am a big HubSpot fanboy and I just love their business model, I'd say that reciprocity does not need to be leveraged purposefully if it's a built-in trait of today's successful businesses.

Teach. Give to get.

A helpful and educational resource promotes meaning.

"All the gold which is under or upon the earth is not enough to give in exchange for virtue."

(PLATO)

THE LAW OF TIME

Changing someone's time perspective helps them to make different decisions. When people change their time perspective, they change how they feel about something and the decision they make in regard to it.

People will behave differently depending on whether their primary time orientation is present, past, or future. Human civilization is set apart from the natural timing frequency. This law governs the universal order, whereas the artificial timing frequency sets modern synchronization apart from the biosphere.

Humans created time as we know; it is not ruled by the biosphere. It is a technological invention. The watch is a machine invented to measure events occurring in time. We live by the clock, we are born by the clock, and we are used to it. It is said that time travel is not possible. This is wrong. In our minds we can. We have memories and we have dreams. We can anticipate events and plan. The future is not a dark place. We invent it and we actualize it at our will.

We can picture ourselves in the future and we can create images in other people's heads. It is all about how you make others feel about something by altering their time perception. Picture people vividly in their happy future and anticipate what you want by painting it clearly in your public's mind. Zoom them forward and further into the future by engaging them in consequential thinking over long-term dreams. You must be able to create and motivate change by creating compelling visions and showing people what they will be like in a bright future, jumping ahead and indulging a fallacious and illusive sense of time by directing and channeling thoughts.

The subjective sense of time is a huge part of our life. We do often travel in the future and anticipate regret for not having done something. We create distorted frames of mind that are just perceptions of reality itself. Describing vividly how your outcome will be experienced by others in the future is often referred to as *future pacing*. In simple words, it's distorting time by drawing pictures in people's minds, helping them to get frustrated with their present conditions and happy about anything else—helping them envision a bright and new vision versus their current mediocre status.

Interruptive marketing is obsolete and no longer cost-effective. Inbound Marketing is the future.

THE LAW OF ASSOCIATION

We tend to like products, services, and ideas that are endorsed by other people we like or respect.

To quote Zig Ziglar, *"People want to either be at the top, be seen with the people on the top or be given hope that they might be able to be at the top."* To make up meanings, our minds link everything. Everything is associated and compared in relation to other things. We associate, we compare, we contrast. Provided that it feels like it, anything can be related to everything. Advertisers use association a lot by linking their products and services to famous and successful people who radiate fame and fortune.

Music, aroma, fragrances, sounds, images, and words have the power to elicit feelings. Symbols have the same (if not stronger) power. The wedding ring, the Crucifix, the Swastika, and the Hammer and Sickle arouse powerful feelings in people's minds.

The world is too complex for our limited capacity of processing information. For this particular reason, the average person lives by learned stereotypes in order to make sense of things. Despite the fact that some experts say that the validity of using famous people as testimonials is no longer tempting (and too expensive), it is worth considering that, if your products and services (and even you) are linked to likable and positively famous people, the chances of success increase.

In NLP, the anchoring process is used to capture and re-propose conditioned feelings, emotions, and even memories. Unquestionably, we live a semantic and symbolic life, and associations are a powerful tool. You need to capture people's minds with positive feelings and states of mind and not let any negative feeling, emotion, or memory be associated with you.

Never.

THE LAW OF CONTRAST

When two things, people, or places that are relatively different from each other are placed near each other in time and space or thought, we will see them as more different, making it is easier to distinguish which one we desire the most.

As human beings we always try to make sense of things.

We make judgments on the basis of associating things and making comparisons. Contrast is the difference between two or more elements. Our perceptions are deeply affected when we are introduced to different alternatives in succession. As American novelist Herman Melville once said, *"There is no quality in this world that is not what it is merely by contrast. Nothing exists in itself."* We make purchasing decisions comparing products and services, and we even judge people in contrast to other people.

Apparently, this is strictly related to our preprogramming since we were kids, especially when it all comes down to pricing issues. On the other hand, the issue is not always about pricing. People usually choose the less expensive options and tend to better remember the last thing they saw. The former depends on how people view money and their financial power (*and, OK, the majority will go for the less expensive item*), while the latter is scientifically proven to be true.

In 1996, I was a college student in Australia. I went to check out a retail estate agent to find a flat to rent. To influence my decision process, I was shown two disgusting flats that could resemble the worst jails shown on TV. According to what I was looking for, it was pretty certain I'd never live there. The third was a nice flat that mirrored my criteria. Compared to a prison, it was a huge improvement.

Another trick to gain compliance is to show the expensive item first and then, as a second option, discuss what you want to sell (usually a less expensive option), but contrasting does not stop here. The sales executive who sold my first business suit to me said, "*Your CHF850 suit choice is absolutely fantastic; you might wish to consider purchasing this fabulous (and necessary) tie. It marries perfectly with your new suit, and it is only CHF59, and you'd surely like to see a nice pair of shoes that seem just to be produced for that particular business suit!*" I bought everything.

The very same principle can be applied to the restaurant industry. No wonder the waitress takes your dessert order at the end of your meal. Compared to your romantic dinner, a CHF15 lemon with vodka sorbet is not so expensive, is it?

Our innate mechanism of associating and contrasting can be applied to everything, even favors. I may ask you a huge favor I know you will never comply with and then a smaller one that you surely will comply with.

Contrast is an essential part of the online world. Effective web design and making differences apparent and visible is key to the business process. With billions of offers offline and online, a key fundamental of any marketing technique is differentiation. Positioning is all about contrast and comparison to other brands.

This does not mean to offer a large number of options or choices that may lead to confusion and cognitive dissonance when faced with too many alternatives. It means to be different.

Make differences apparent.

Visible.

THE LAW OF FRIENDS (CONNECTING, RELATING, AND COOPERATING)

When someone asks you to do something and you perceive that person has your best interest in mind, and/or you would like him/her to have your best interest in mind, you are strongly motivated to fulfill the request.

When it comes to your publics, you should always appeal to as many people as possible, considering connections and relationships (groups of interest, friends, and family). People are preprogrammed to care about their families, friends, and peers (other than themselves). We all want and need to feel wanted. Customers and prospects are no exception. They are people like us and need to be taken care of by others who truly care about them.

This attitude to try to tie people down is often used by multilevel marketers who astutely use the "friends and family strategy" to reach their goals. We like things familiar and we dramatically increase the probability of compliance if we are seen as someone who cares—a friend. Even negative aspects of the product or service shall be pointed out to set the target at ease and gain trust.

The more we feel attracted to and liked by others, the more persuasive they become. We prefer to comply to requests from people we like, and, many times, we purchase solely on a recommendation from a trusted friend, colleague, or family member. A friend will tell a friend.

A friend is someone who is truly interested in you—a loyal person who respects you and shows empathy without pushing. We all love similarity and familiarity. We like those who are like us in some way. This can be based on a multitude of commonalities, such as education, hobbies, professional interests, passions, et cetera.

Being liked is vital in today's world, and it is the core prerequisite for the influence process. Referring to people by their first name (depending on the context) might increase likability, and the use of humor in an appropriate manner does the very same thing. If one is genuinely caring, kind, and respectful of others, there should be no drama in being liked. The solution is to be transparent and trustworthy, to make people feel comfortable around you, and to create trust by being truly and sincerely interested in others.

Relationships influence meanings.

THE LAW OF EXPECTANCY

When someone you respect and/or believe in expects you to perform a task or produce a certain result, you will tend to fulfill his or her expectations whether positive or negative.

Meaning-attribution to expectations creates reality as self-fulfilling prophecies. If you think you will fail, you surely will.

The myth says that there are tribes who exceed a hundred years. They are called Long Livers, and they are a mystery. Some say that they grow old and live longer because they do not have any expectation with regard to their age.

We behave as we are classified by the societal set—as others expect us to. Expectation is powerful and may radically alter performance and change behaviors. We all have expectations. Others have expectations from us. We tend to follow their thinking and do our best to fulfill the expectations. Do you remember when your parents expected you to go to the best college and/or university and get that well-paid job in public administration?

If I am a coach and expect a lot from you, and I know that you will perform accordingly at your best. The contrary is also true. However, we need to be very careful when doing our best trying to please someone. People's expectations are not always the best for us. In life, it's like we are given a role and we feel forced to act as expected within the social set. This is especially the case in work settings. If you diminish the value of your employees, they will perform accordingly.

What do you expect from your publics?

Expectations play a very important role in all the areas of our lives. Often, people go along with our proposals on the basis of simple expectations. If you prefer another word for this:

Commitment.

THE LAW OF CONSISTENCY

When an individual announces in writing (or verbally to a lesser degree) that he is taking a position on any issue or point of view, he will strongly tend to defend that belief regardless of its accuracy even in the face of overwhelming evidence of the contrary.

We love consistency. We love congruency. This principle refers to our deep psychological need to be consistent. We live in a knowledge- and information-dense and complex world, and we have to resort to shortcuts and heuristics in order to not be overwhelmed by the burden to think, or worse, to make decisions.

We have an innate desire to be (and/or to appear) consistent with what we have done in the past. In case of a hypothetical commitment made in the past, we will encounter personal and interpersonal pressures to behave consistently to that particular commitment in the future.

Consistency is a powerful motivational tool, whereas inconsistency is not considered a welcomed personality trait. We like consistent people and despise inconsistent individuals. This demonstrates how past choices and proclamations influence people's attitudes and future choices and give us the opportunity to predict behaviors. The reason is fairly simple: people seek consistency and act accordingly to their attitudes, beliefs, and values because it is easier to make decisions based upon past choices; it is not socially-nice to appear inconsistent.

Inconsistency is a self-contradictory proposition that causes internal discomfort, leading to a need to restore our harmonious balance. Cognitive dissonance states that we hold conflicting ideas with regard to our past decisions. We would have to admit that we were wrong and that we made a wrong decision or choice.

Sometimes we simultaneously hold two inconsistent cognitions and find ourselves in a negative state of mind—a state of discomfort. Any feelings of dissonance threaten our self-esteem. We feel guilty, inadequate, and even hypocritical. To reduce the tension we feel, we might deny facts or things; fight to the bitter end to justify our opinions, decisions, actions, and behaviors; or reframe our constructed meanings and admit we were wrong.

We hate dissonance and we do not particularly welcome information that opposes or criticizes our personal point of view. Basically, consistency is an inborn and deep trait of our behavioral and cultural background. We just feel the need to be consistent.

Beliefs and behaviors that are not made public are more likely to change due to future attempts of persuasion. If you gain commitment from someone (in writing, in public, or verbally), you create a sense of obligation and dramatically increase your probabilities of getting a positive reply to future requests. People tend to follow through when committing publicly or in writing. The key is to create involvement and have people engage and commit, triggering self-justification and leveraging the need to comply to restore any hurt feelings.

In marketing and sales, it happens quite often that companies ask for your commitment and then conveniently forget to tell you about some parts of the contract. Most of the time they get away with it. Nowadays, the offers are everywhere, and loyalty must be rewarded. Small commitments often lead to larger ones. Written or public commitments are a strong leverage with reference to consistency. It is quite easy to create dissonance when you get commitment from people by offering solutions and clever calls to action. Once you get written/public commitment, is up to you to play with it.

It is widely suggested to avoid politician-style incongruent behaviors. If the important goal is your diet, it would be inconsistent to celebrate by doing the opposite of what would achieve the goal—eating a Big Mac and washing it down with a jug of beer. Consistency is an important aspect of our behavior. It is important when it comes to writing professionally (avoid inconsistencies in spelling and grammar usage) and to your online presence (avoid strange pictures of that nice party you had at your place; on the web, you are what you publish).

Be genuine and consistent with what you preach.

"Unless commitment is made, there are only promises and hopes; but no plans."

(PETER F. DRUCKER)

THE LAW OF SCARCITY

When people perceive that something they might want is limited in quantity, they believe the value of what they might want to be greater than if it were available in abundance.

!ACT NOW - BUY NOW - LIMITED SUPPLIES -
ONE MONTH ONLY - ONE DAY ONLY -
LAST CHANCE!

!Limited supply versus present economy of use.
No future alternative!

Why does scarcity drive people mad? What does never to being able to find the desired item or that piece of information ever again mean to you?

Diamonds are Forever (1971) is the seventh Agent 007 series film, based on Ian Fleming's novel of the same name—the British author's fourth James Bond series of novels, first published in March 1956. Starring Sean Connery, James Bond impersonates a diamond smuggler in a diamond smuggling investigation that leads him uncover an extortion plot where diamonds are used to build a giant laser.

Diamonds are a valuable commodity and have been jealously treasured as luxurious gemstones, with their image cleverly preserved through astute marketing campaigns since they gained popularity. A large trade of diamonds exists, although the production and distribution is consolidated, at large, in the hands of a few key players.

Black Astrum is a UK-based company that provides products befitting their members' standing in society. Their business cards are crafted to recognize this status and provide a product unique to the selected few, yet they are distinctive to anyone who should receive one. The cards are encrusted in diamonds of the highest quality and are designed to make an immediate statement. Production is limited and offers to new members are by invitation only.

The idea is not new; exclusive business cards made from one hundred percent carbon or silver fiber are already in high demand. The Sotheby's World Élite MasterCard was launched as a premium credit card in 2007; however, this offer seems to go one step further when talking about individuality and luxury. Asian online magazine *Luxury Insider* quoted that you need to have more than money to get these cards, seeing that the company's concept director has turned down several requests already, focusing on the invitation principle and saying that this reflects their desire to serve only the most premier individuals.

Black Astrum is artfully playing on several fields of consumer psychology. Status and esteem are surely important bricks here. Maslow included status in his pyramid-like structure depicting psychological and physical needs, and, despite the static structure of his interpretation, tons of studies and research in sociology, anthropology, and psychology demonstrate that we all desire to be well-respected and that the honor or prestige attached to one's position in society is considered extremely important to many.

The price of this business card, studded with diamonds and Swiss materials, is available upon request. Invitation is needed. What is the meaning of this strategy? Individuality, exclusivity, and luxury are variables that we already know quite well. However, at a psychological level, one might notice that the Law of Scarcity is masterfully used here.

In the diamond industry, this law was used in the past. DeBeers, could maintain a monopoly over the demand supply managing to render the diamonds purposefully scarce. The company ran only ten diamond sales a year and invited only a selected number of dealers (only giving them a limited amount of diamonds upon selective practices) to maintain tight control over supplies and pricing.

In a document published by the World Diamond Council, it was written that diamonds have been used throughout history as a symbol to express emotions, and they are desirable to consumers because they hold deep emotional meaning, are one of the earth's most precious creations, are unique, and will last for eternity.

The more we have, the more we want. We always want more and scarcity increases the value of any product or service. Soon enough (unfortunately) we will run out of drinkable water. Water wars to grab the last drop between big corporations have already begun some time ago.

Letting your client know that something about you or your offer is scarce (e.g. time, quantity, information) pulls the emotional triggers to act immediately. Deadlines, exclusive offers, and hard-to-collect items trigger action. Clever calls to action should play with the fear of potential loss. No one likes fear. We all dislike loss and restrictions to freedom.

"I never hated a man enough to give him diamonds back."

(ZSA ZSA GABOR)

THE LAW OF CONFORMITY AND SOCIAL VALIDATION

Most people tend to agree to proposals, products, or services that will be perceived as acceptable by the majority or a majority of the individual's peer group.

Individuals fear loneliness. We are a social species and we feel an innate drive to belong and to be accepted by others. Conformity is strictly related to consistency; in fact, most people tend to be sensitive and consistent with the ideas of their group, or the group they would like to belong to, for the desire of identification and the group's acceptance.

An idea or a trend may be contagious and affect many people with the help of this principle. The more we see people doing something, the more we believe it is correct to do it. Fundamentally, we try to figure things out by watching what other people do in order to understand what is socially acceptable by the majority.

The most downloaded eBook, the most tweeted article, and the most popular or best-selling item increases the chance that people act and do the very same thing. We validate our behavior by following unwritten social norms. By playing with time and letting your publics see a bright future after buying the product or service, where their families, peers, and friends are excited about the purchase, you will increase the probabilities to sell. On the contrary, a fake audience or comments are not suggested seeing that online communities (and offline people as well) are quite good in spotting misleading behaviors. One should provide proof that the product or service is in high demand. You are the place to be and you are the fastest-growing company in your industry because you are the very best.

It all comes down to having a sound understanding of your audience's decision-making processes and offering them great solutions by genuinely helping them make meaningful decisions and be healthier choosers. They will look good in front of their peers, they will feel better, and they will be happy.

They will reciprocate.

THE LAW OF POWER

People have power over other people to the degree that they are perceived as having greater authority, strength, or expertise in contrast to others.

The vast majority of people act in their interest. Everyone wants more power. To quote Napoleon Bonaparte, "*To have ultimate victory, you must be ruthless.*" Everyone is power hungry and the struggle for power reminds us of a jungle. Power is something most people have desired since antiquity. It comes with authority and charisma. It is the ability to change and alter behaviors.

Titles, status, hierarchy, financial resources, and the like all contribute in being perceived by others as more powerful. People are out for a race to the top, and no one really cares (or wishes) to be found at the bottom.

Power is a double-edged knife and should be used *with* people (as charisma), not over them. You should make it known by showing (not telling and acting as a know-it-all jerk) that you are the best among the top within your area of expertise. You are a thoughtful leader, an authority, and the must-go-to resource.

Over time, life has not changed much. Everything is still judged by appearances, and being lost in the crowd of inferior status never counts to other people, hence the need to act with comfort and confidence but not with visible disregard and conceit. Power is important, but, in the modern world we live in, it might be seen as a dangerous quality. For this particular reason, true intentions shall be concealed by constant strategic thinking and covert moves.

"Always mystify, mislead, and surprise the enemy, if possible. Such tactics will win every time and a small army may thus destroy a large one."

(GENERAL STONEWALL JACKSON)

SIMPLICITY

Do you remember when you were a little kid and used to hate some classes that you considered daunting and useless at the same time?

Math is a classic example. It is difficult, challenging, demanding, and laboriously painful—a problem. Playfully, we could easily infer that the main problem of a problem lies in its negative connotation. We all grew up with total certainty that every challenge we face in our lives is to be considered a problem. We grew up with negative feelings associated with this word and we might have suffered, or suffer, from this assertion.

Life is challenging means that life is a problem—a cause-effect false assertion.

In cartoons and in the virtual life, we might use the magic wand. We can't do so in the real world, even though we all wish we could. Every day we might face challenges and difficulties related to our business and private lives. This does not necessarily mean being overwhelmed by futile problems.

Notwithstanding the real implications of health issues, hunger, wars, and the like, it is to be highlighted that most of us, in Western cultures, just follow the path of a frivolous human tendency, sometimes dictated by controversial philosophers, movements, and folklorist disciplines of the past, building up extremely complex meanings from simplicity.

We see problems everywhere. And, if there are none, we do our best to create some. We live in the meaning economy, not in a mathematically complex system model reality, where extremely complicated information shall be meticulously deciphered. Every problem asks for a solution. When facing a problem, we should be asking ourselves if this problem is a problem in the first place. It all lies in the semantics. And remember, before we can change anything, we must recognize the source of the problem first, not the symptoms, and the meaning we attach to things in our minds.

"Simplicity is the ultimate sophistication."

(LEONARDO DA VINCI)

LIE TO ME

Sometimes, the truth is unpleasant. Most of the time we lie to make others feel good, and, at the same time, we usually tend to believe and have faith in what others tell us.

With lying, trust is always at stake.

Body language is not easy to fake. True feelings are signaled involuntarily, and that is why we need to develop self-awareness and the necessary sensory acuity by sharpening our senses through observation and listening skills.

We communicate with everything—with our dress, eye contact, facial expressions, posture, body movements, and online content. We use words to communicate information, and, at the same time, we convey feelings, emotions, and attitudes by body language. Meaning is derived mostly by non-verbal cues. As appearance, our body language should be appropriate to the context and congruent with what we actually say. People make snap decisions whether they trust, like, believe, want to date, have sex with, work with, or do business with us. It's just a matter of seconds— a glance.

Facial expressions display a variety of emotions, and it is widely accepted that there are six recognizable emotions: Happiness, Sadness, Surprise, Disgust, Fear, and Anger. Furthermore, we convey signals of comfort or discomfort and anxiety by validating our message with our body language (open or closed body language) and other particular traits. For example, we display the following uncontrollable habits when we experience tension: head scratching, tugging earlobes, fingers in the nose (yuk!), or some strange micro-facial contortions of ours that might demonstrate/validate inner conflict and frustration.

One does not need to be as crazy as many practitioners and become a pain for others by looking and judging every movement they make. It really all depends on the context—the congruence of words versus behavior and clusters of gestures.

> *"If you want to tell lies that will be believed do not tell the truth that won't."*
> *Emperor Tokugawa Ieyasu of Japan*

TRUE LISTENING

People hate to listen, as they hate to read. People love to talk, especially about themselves.

Active listening skills are a must in the influence process. Through our body language, we can demonstrate to our interlocutor that we are truly listening and showing empathy. For example, with head nods (to acknowledge approval, understanding, or encouragement by nodding your head up and down or to show disapproval by shaking the head from one side to the other) and with eye contact (not a distracted gaze), we can show people that they have our complete attention. You would not like to talk with someone who's looking around all the time, would you?

Listening is a psychological process and differs from hearing, which is physiological. The key here is to be able to listen and gather vital intelligence. What is meaningful to your interlocutor?

It is not so difficult to attain a thorough knowledge of the individual.

Ask and pay attention by being interested.

Listen to your publics.

GIVE ME YOUR EYES THAT I MIGHT SEE

Leonardo Da Vinci believed that the eyes are the window of the soul. Leading experts are still trying to discover what the *Mona Lisa* is conveying with her enigmatic eyes. Others believe that body language is a window to our minds.

There is a great deal of research into understanding eye movements with regard to the fascinating relationship with our internal representations. Beginning with original research in the 1950s, psychologist Ernest Hilgard distinguished himself through his studies of the role of hypnosis in human behavior and response-ability. He was interested in how eye movements related to behavior, and he did extensive research with the human eyelid.

In the 1970s, Grinder and Bandler did further research to explore the relationship between eye movements and the different sensory modalities, as well as other different cognitive processes. Within NLP, the various senses are considered as information processors and are known as sensory modalities.

The following list includes our sensory-specific modalities:

- Visual: sights, images
- Auditory: sounds, speech, dialogue
- Kinesthetic: feelings, emotions
- Olfactory: smell
- Gustatory: taste

Eye accessing cues: As agreed by many, eye movements as indicators of cognitive processes is one of the most well-known and valuable discoveries of NLP. When people think, their eyes move in particular, patterned directions. Bandler wrote that he was puzzled about the fact that psychology never discovered this fact and that he probably noticed because he approached human behavior as an information scientist and not as a psychologist. Eyes may or may not be the windows to our souls, but they are surely interrelated with our emotions, feelings, and responses. The eyes do not lie and reveal a great deal of information about what is happening inside our bodies and minds. Research tells us the following:

LOOKING TO THE RIGHT

- UP (Visually Constructed = constructing images, something never seen)
- LEVEL (Auditory Constructed = constructing sound and/or words, never heard before)
- DOWN (Kinesthetic Feelings = sensing inner past or future feelings)

LOOKING TO THE LEFT

- UP (Visually Remembered = seen before, remembering)
- LEVEL (Auditory Remembered = sounds and/or words from the past, remembering)
- DOWN (Auditory Digital = internal dialogue, self talk)

Eye movement cues can be easily observed. These movements might be habitual but for sure are a part of our body language that cannot be consciously controlled. This gives important cues on a person's preferred sensory modality system and can be a leading detector for either truth or deception.

Eyes are the focal pit of the face, and emotions rush out from them. We might express liking and intimacy, exercise control and submission, and provide information and regulate interpersonal interactions.

The eyes play a big part in creating rapport and establishing trust and credibility.

The eyes never lie.

Other important factors:

Any contact in the eye-nose triangle is considered eye contact.

Usually, in business settings it is suggested to focus on the forehead with base corners coinciding with the eyes. In social relations, the focus should be a little lower, whereas in intimacy the focus is to discretely scan from the eyes to just below the chin in a flirtatious manner.

Staring frequently (holding contact few seconds longer than normal) might display interest. On the other hand, gazing too much can result in making people uncomfortable, and minimal contact might display confusion, boredom, distraction, or no attention to the interlocutor.

The best solution would be to make intelligent eye contact (about two-thirds of the time) depending on the context and to be very careful of cultural differences. Eye contact is important in Western cultures (lowering eyes, for instance is a submissive and non-confident gesture), whereas it is a form of disrespect in Japan.

The human blinking rate is usually around fifteen times a minute. A more rapid blinking rate might be due to annoying lights, stress or pressure, anxiety, or lying.

Eyebrow flashes are a common trait to most cultures in the world.

Pupils grow larger when we are frightened or attracted to someone.

We like people with clear eyes, meaning that blood-shot eyes or bags under the eyes show that you do not get enough sleep or that you party too much. Sunglasses are another sign of distrust; in fact, subconsciously we are not keen to trust people wearing sunglasses because we believe that they are hiding something from us by not allowing us to see their eyes.

"The eyes are the mirror of the soul."

(YIDDISH PROVERB)

CAN I ASK YOU A FAVOR?

Smile.

Smiling is an easy yet extremely important task. As each one of us can notice just by looking around, very few people smile. Generally, there is no time to smile because we're in a hurry, and we do not consider it important, nor do we care much about the habit of smiling.

First of all, we know that we are always in some state of mind. It could not be otherwise. Much research has been done with regard to facial expressions and a lot of it on smiling. Why? Because smiling appears to be infectious and contagious. Clearly, it needs to be a natural and spontaneous smile. A fake does not produce the same effect.

Smiling is strictly related to behavior. A smile has the power to impact our emotions and other attitudes. A genuine and congruent smile encourages a positive interaction. Take Thailand, for instance. It is a very popular destination for many travelers, and it is affectionately known as the "Land of Smiles." No wonder that ninety-five percent of the Thai population is Buddhist. People are more than ready to smile as a reflection of Buddha's teachings on the subject.

Without even saying a word, people immediately know if we are engaging in some effort to put a smile on our faces or if we are displaying a real smile. Displaying happiness equals a happy smile. Incongruent smiles just do not work as well and are easily spotted. Smiling affects our emotions/feelings and others' emotions/feelings about us.

In the business arena, people are taught to smile prior to answering the phone. The reason? Try it. Try to smile before picking up your phone when someone is calling. You'll feel the difference in your whole body and in your tone of voice. It just feels much different and it is perceived as such.

Politicians are experts at this. They do always smile, don't they? Smiling works, especially if you are genuine. It works in the influence and persuasion process and it makes you a more agreeable person for others to gravitate to.

Make a genuine and warm smile a habit of yours.

"Sometimes your joy is the source of your smile, but sometimes your smile can be the source of your joy."
Thích Nhất Hạnh

THE ART OF THE EIGHT LIMBS

Muay Thai is the "Art of Eight Limbs" or the "Science of Eight Limbs." It makes use of punches, kicks, and elbows and knee strikes, thus using eight "points of contact" as opposed to "two points" (fists) in boxing and "four points" (hands and feet) used in other more regulated combat sports, such as kickboxing.

Thus, it is the direct ancestor of modern Thai boxing; Muay boran is not a single style but acts as an umbrella term for all traditional Thai styles of Indochinese kickboxing. Muay boran is said to make use of *nawa awut* which means "nine weapons," adding headbutts as a ninth offensive "tool" in addition to the "eight limbs" masterfully used in modern ring fights.

Our gestures and how we displace our limbs make up our body language and convey meaning to other people. Self-comfort or frenzied gestures associated with our limbs leak our information and give away our feelings to people who are able to read our movements. Physiology includes all the inner and outer behaviors of our neurology system, which activates motor programs (glands/neurology/emotions); this includes some external factors, such as the quality of our resting (sleep), our patterns of exercise, and, on the whole, our health.

Hands: Research shows that the neurological connection between our brain and our hands is greater than other limbs. Some cultures have the habit of gesturing a lot and accompany their speeches with hand movements—others not so much. However, it is strongly suggested to always keep your hands away from your face (and even from your butt) and never point your index finger to people. Most of the time, we are unaware of what we're doing. When I am in a deep thinking mood, I keep stroking my chin. This is an example of unconscious behavior, such as touching lips, eating nails, and other similar behaviors.

Psychologically, from ancient times, empty hands are considered less aggressive than fists. Fists are for fighting whereas empty palms semantically mean that you have no weaponry in your hands. This is a bit pretentious seeing that empty hands might lead to more damage to your opponent in a close combat situation, but, as we know, emotions are much stronger than logic when it comes to our unconscious thinking. Political advisers know these tricks very well. They always tell their clients to be palms up (palms down is considered to issue commands) and stress the importance of an energetic and firm handshake.

Arms: Are you a bouncer? Just imagine your last evening out. Have you noticed that bouncers usually fold their arms across their chests? Crossed arms are perceived as being a defense barrier and are usually interpreted as being negative. Crossed arms may also show discomfort, whereas partial arm cross displaces inner nervous energy coming out. As a result, if you are not a bad ass be careful about crossing arms.

In wintertime, it might be that you cross your arms because you are freezing. Remember, it all depends on the context.

Feet: In Thai culture, feet are considered the most unclean part of the body. Pointing your feet to someone, or to a Buddha statue, is regarded as very rude behavior. In our Westernized society, things are slightly different. We have the tendency to go toward pleasure, and we do our best to turn away from pain. As a consequence, if legs or feet are pointed away from you, and not in line with the body posture of your interlocutor, it means the other person just desires to leave.

Legs: Crossed legs signals must be taken with chopsticks, especially when it comes to women. Crossing legs may be for comfort purposes, depending on the clothing. Generally speaking, either for women and men, crossed arms plus crossed legs during a meeting is a trouble indicator.

We're not grappling on a ring: Our private and personal space is vital. It is important to note that we can find ourselves in crowded situations in business and social settings. Few of us are Muay Thai or Brazilian Ju-Jitsu practitioners; this means that we shall always respect other people's space. A handshake distance is usually OK, but it really depends on the context. It is argued that, at a subconscious level, we like to be touched. On the other hand, we must be very careful because some hate it, and in some cultures touch is very disrespectful. A light physical touch to areas such as hands, forearms and shoulders, depending on the context and the relationship with the interlocutor, is usually more than fine.

ARE WE IN SYNC?

The ability to influence others is dictated by others liking and trusting you, by the meanings they made up about you, and by being in sync. Most of the time, this is an _unconscious process_. You need to be able to accurately synchronize everything to appeal to your audience.

Like attracts like. We tend to like the most those people who like us and who are like us. Rapport is all about affinity;

it is about creating a psychological bridge with someone leading to positive responses in the social setting. An old saying byword narrates that *the birds of the same species fly together.* This is true. We are a social species and we do enjoy mixing with people who are just like us; instead, we desire to associate with people who genuinely share our values, our beliefs, and our interests.

Sometimes this just happens. We like someone without even knowing the reason. Other times, this process might be leveraged with intention. As a matter of fact, all of us like to talk about what we love and what we know. If you talk with somebody without caring about these two factors, you'll probably end up annoying your interlocutor. People like to talk about what they like/love/know and about themselves. Here lies the importance to true listening to gather intelligence.

Emphasis shall be put on the fact that sincere empathy, curiosity, and a genuine interest in what others have to say is vital to this process. If you just do not care or you do not have any clear outcome in mind, it would be pointless. Some say it is incredibly important to create rapport, but this does not mean to exaggerate as some NLP practitioners do. Rapport is not mimicking.

Rapport with our words using VAKOG: By paying attention to what others have to say, we can easily discover their representational systems. Our various senses play their roles as our information processors, and our way of talking is the result of how we see the world. If I say "*I see your point,*" this differs quite a lot from "*I hear your point.*" There is a great difference in the *sensory modality* used to create my map of the world. By aligning ourselves to someone else's system, we tend to increase the probabilities of being in sync.

Leveraging rapport by pacing (and leading): Pacing involves establishing rapport and harmony to make persuasive communication much easier. Then, as in dancing, comes leading. And following. It's all about being liked because we're alike.

With our voice and language: Our words are carried out by our voices. By vocal pacing we can get even better results. We can "speak the same" by adjusting our speed, volume (heights/lows), speech rate, and tone of voice to the person we are dealing with.

Speaking the same language (*in general*) is also very important. Using similar lingo instead of industry jargon is stressed in any industry setting.

Pacing with our voice requires minor adjustments in order to match speed, rhythm, tone, and even accents being careful not to frustrate people or sounding foolish, or worse, make fun of your interlocutor.

Vocal cues: Our vocal tone is different if we compare a lullaby to a Striiike! or Goooalllll! The way (and how) we say things is crucial. People tend to speak at a consistent rate with how they are processing their thoughts and internal representations. As a consequence, it is a good idea to place emphasis on different words, inflection and volume, and pauses and tonality by avoiding professor-like monotones.

Vocal cues are quite difficult to grasp because we do not know our voices. If you ever get a chance, record yourself speaking and listen to your voice. You'll be amazed to hear yourself talking. The important thing is to express confidence (you are looking out for credibility); therefore, it is strongly suggested not to be shy, not to express fear (with a trembling voice), and to avoid repeating the same words or make strange sounds like *Uh! Ah! Ehm!*

Unless you are used to it, it is not easy to speak in front of people let alone in front of a camera. It is very different than speaking to one single interlocutor. The energy levels are very different and you should be able to match them. Experience helps. Trial and error is the beginning.

Breathing: This is a very elegant and powerful way to create rapport. Experts argue that during meditation, sex, and hypnotherapy, we breathe at the same rate as our partner. This process is not as easy as pacing with our voices; it takes practice to be able to adjust our breathing style to others.

The trick is to be able to focus and observe your prospect's chest as in martial arts.

Physiology and posture: There are two ways to adjust our bodies and align our movements and body image to build rapport. Mirroring happens when you adopt the same type of body behavior. After a handful of seconds, you adjust your posture (e.g. if your interlocutor crosses the left leg, you cross the right one). On the other hand, Matching is pretty similar. The only difference is that, if we take into account the previous example, when your interlocutor crosses the left leg, you cross your left leg.

Mirroring and Matching shall not be done immediately after your interlocutor takes action. You do not want to fool yourself by making others uncomfortable or allowing them point you out.

The natural consequence of pacing is then leading to see if you are in rapport (or not). In this particular instance, you can lead with your voice (_tone, rate, speed_) or your body behavior (_physiology and posture_) and check out if your interlocutor does the very same thing.

In you have a follower, you have rapport. On the contrary, if you do not, you shall repeat the process.

"Take care to get what you like or you will be forced to like what you get."

(George Bernard Shaw)

THE WORLD IS NOT ENOUGH

The web is the primary and unquestioned source of information and networking.

We live in a knowledge- and information-intense digital era. The current worldwide economic conditions seem to be persistently volatile. There are fewer vacancies. The competition is fierce. The web developments and possibilities seem to be endless. There are plenty of new digital channels offering the chance to virtually contact everyone everywhere on the planet.

New ways to interact. New ways to get found. New ways to meet people. New ways to date. New ways to meet potential employers. New ways to convey meaning. The web is a gold mine of opportunities to be exploited, regardless of your field of expertise. It is just a forgotten cave if you are invisible.

Marketing PRopaganda is the ability to make concepts into words and symbols of great significance—the creation of meaning to be impressed into the public's mind. It is concerned with shifting and changing the mental pictures of the world in people's heads by appealing to individuals by means of every possible approach, securing trust and loyalty of key people and intentionally motivating the audience to accept whatever needs to be brought to acceptance.

Meaning is the most critical factor in human nature.

"Branding adds spirit and a soul to what would otherwise be a robotic, automated, generic price-value proposition. If branding is ultimately about the creation of human meaning, it follows logically that it is the humans who must ultimately provide it."

(DAVID A. AAKER)

TROP DE CHOIX TUE LE CHOIX

This is a French saying that highlights the paradox about choice—too many choices kill the choice.

University of California professor Daniel L. McFadden was quoted by *The Economist* as saying *that consumers find too many options troubling because of the "risk of misperception and miscalculation, of misunderstanding the available alternatives, of misreading one's own tastes, of yielding to a moment's whim and regretting it afterwards" combined with "the stress of information acquisition."*

Too much choice/information will result in a mind-overload, which creates confusion and might result in no buying decision and a concept or idea not being positively welcomed. The human mind has limited capacity for information processing. Too much information and too many choices cause stress and lead people to rely on heuristics and biases to arrive at a choice. Not choosing is also considered a choice.

In decision-making analysis, recognition heuristics are used where people have to choose between two options and between two competing products. If one is recognized and the other not, the choice is easily made. In this knowledge-, information-, and people-oriented and global economy, the presence of infobesity has become the norm; added to simultaneous choice, multiple objectives, time, and other constraints, decision-making is likely to be widely biased.

With multiple choices available, the unaided individual might encounter difficulties. For this reason, companies should focus on quality, valuable content, and helping out their audience to solve problems by over-delivering on expectations.

Perception management is not to be underestimated and is strictly associated with the scientific principle of priming. Recognition has always been an important topic, whereas reputation and familiarity will increase probabilities in terms of converting prospects into qualified leads and loyal customers.

To construct a solid reputation and an invincible goodwill, organizations need to become restless meaning creators and enrich their publics' lives with the highest possible meanings embodied to fulfilling their dreams and helping them better govern their lives.

"It takes 20 years to build a reputation and five minutes to ruin it. If you think about that, you'll do things differently."

(WARREN E. BUFFETT)

ONLINE NEUROSCIENCE

Millions of people are online. Neuroscience is the study of the nervous system. Added to the online world, it means to focus on user intent and to understand behaviors and motives. There are many historical recurrences of advertisers returning to human, social, and behavioral sciences to either unearth human needs, wants, and desires through detailed behavioral analyses or to better mold their targeted messages.

In 2011, Facebook sponsored a Neuro-Marketing study run by Nielsen company Neurofocus. According to Neurofocus Founder and CEO, Dr. A.K. Pradeep, *"Understanding the human brain is truly the ultimate frontier."*

In the joint study, researchers focused on key conscious and subconscious elements of how consumers respond explicitly/implicitly to sensory experiences along three core dimensions—Attention, Emotion, and Memory (which are considered as being universal responses)—the degree to which either messages and conceptual associations are strengthened by an experience, and testing scores on overall neurological effectiveness (A composite score that combines the three core dimensions' responses in a sole measure. In other words, the overall cognitive impact of the website-viewing experience).

To find out any significant pattern, the participants' brainwaves were measured throughout the experience with their own Facebook page, Yahoo! and The New York Times homepages. Between non-personalized Yahoo! (lightly informational and entertainment-oriented), The New York Times (highly informational, but neither personal nor social), and Facebook (social, personal, and informational), researchers' findings indicate that:

- ATTENTION is overall significant, with no particular (positive or negative) distinction with regard to advertisement presence.
- EMOTIONAL ENGAGEMENT is lower than attention and indicates a negative correlation with it. High levels of attention diminish emotional engagement, highlighting that online content asks for more attention/cognitive resources than passive, traditional media (e.g. TV).

- MEMORY processing is triggered by personal significance (e.g. Facebook feeds) or highly informational
content, if compared to less personal/informational
sites.

The study concludes by saying that before the modern
web-tools (social networks) came along, TV was considered
a passive/emotional medium in comparison to the active/
cognitive (but less emotional) online sphere. Tech developments, added to the availability of the highly personalized
and social online experience, shifted the formula to more
engaging online activities. These findings suggest that online
reputation management is categorically imperative. As in the
real world, expectations play a vital role in people's minds,
and, in this era dominated by infobesity, it is extremely important to offer highly relevant, quality information through a
socially personalized (total consumer) experience.

Squeezing meaningful, timely, and emotionally loaded
PRopaganda through the channels of thought is vital to
earn attention, trigger memory processing, and direct decision-making processes.

AWAKENING CURIOSITY (WITH INFORMATION CONVENIENTLY DISPLAYED)

Popular wisdom says that you should never ask a question
that does not lead or get to your wished and desired answer.
Lawyers do this all the time. They convey information via
questioning as an indirect method of directing thoughts.
They are masters of subtly conveying information.

Without curiosity you get no attention. No knowledge.
No meaning. No engagement. No action. No relationships.

Nothing.

Usually, individuals and masses do not even know how they know what they know or what they think they know. People are stereotyped and biased, and most of them don't bother much with knowing.

Questions awaken curiosity, elicit replies, and stimulate the listener to think about an answer. This is quite different from telling people what to do, and it is a fantastic way to convey prepackaged information, which leads to elegantly encouraging others to think about your architected way.

Place your desired outcome into your questions; language has its systematic rules.

As does human behavior.

THE ARCHITECTED WAY

Parkour is a French training method focused on speed and efficiency when faced with obstacles and urban environments. Conversely, in supermarkets and stores, you are forced to follow a route to check out the assortment.

Just think about IKEA. They have smart-planned their shops.

They architected your way.

Thoughts arise from how people choose to think. How can you architect your messages to direct thinking processes toward your desired outcome?

THE NEED TO KNOW

Asking is a great way to gather intelligence, but no one in the world likes the Grand Inquisitors.

Meta Model questioning asks for precision and clarity. Actively listening and inviting more specificity are at the core of the model to gather specific information by chunking down to specifics as opposed to hypnotic language, which works the other way around (chunking up).

A sound knowledge of your publics, their entourage, and their circle of friends and relationships in the social set is part of analyzing the anatomy of your audience's beliefs, values, hopes, dreams, and perceptual filters.

Knowing the anatomy of your audience is the very first step in every area of life. To succeed in influencing people's minds, you need to know them. It is basilar to know your public minds' dynamics, mental filters, and decision-making processes to architect their meaning-making habits.

META PROGRAMS

We all have our own style of perceiving things. It is very important not to undervalue this when profiling buyer personas. We are all different and we all have our own mental filters with which we see and perceive all sorts of information by processing our thoughts. These perceptual sorting patterns often habituate and become our default styles of thinking and perceiving.

One needs to develop active listening and sensory channels awareness in order to grab an understanding on how people make decisions. Knowing how people make up their meanings is vital to communicating more effectively and being able to persuade others. As a preliminary remark, consumers buy what they want. It is no longer merely a matter of necessity. In Westernized societies, it's all about desires.

Do you really need a Louis Vuitton purse?

Often marketers mash up needs and wants without making any distinction. There is a great difference instead. It is fundamental to appeal to people's meanings, guide them in their decision process, and not forget to help them justify their purchase after the deal is made.

Meta programs are perceptual and unconscious filters that direct our subjective experience and behavior. They are the glasses with which we see life in general. To persuade and influence others, we must understand how other people's individual programs work and be able to present our offers in the best possible way to fit their model of the world and their thinking strategies.

Some argue that meta programs are personality traits and that Carl Jung discovered them in the twentieth century, naming them *temperaments.* In the 50s Isabel and Kathryn Myers summarized Jung's typing themes into the Myers-Briggs Type Indicator (MBTI). The problem with MBTI is a common one; as with hundreds of other models, the underlying assumption is that those are permanent traits. They are not static; nothing is. Our thinking, emoting, and perceiving are not static, nor are our personalities.

Meta programs are dynamic and fluid processes that we use to structure our realities. The quest is to get insight into how people operate and think in their unique complexity. People operate according to how they have created their meanings and how they filter information.

We all have unique processes of mind, unique Matrices.

We are egoistic to make assumptions and think that we know all about another's thinking. We might notice verbal and non-verbal cues, but we might not guess the complex programs used to map reality. As Lippmann wrote, "*We shall assume that what each man does is based not on direct and certain knowledge, but on pictures made by himself or given to him*"; here's the extreme importance of meaning-creation strategies and PRopaganda.

Meta programs depend on the socio-eco-cultural context; we internally re-present ideas and experiences through our filtering system, and, by doing so, we supply content and new meanings to our states of mind. There are over fifty patterns that are very useful, but, not being mind readers and knowing that these processes are not static, we imperatively need to be open to actively listening before making any cheap second-guess about other people.

Paradoxically, to learn about the public mind, one needs to avoid patterned and stereotyped shortcuts.

META PROGRAMS IN USE

Are you a masochist? We have the innate tendency to go toward pleasure and to avoid pain. No one likes pain, unless your reply was positive. This is a common way of filtering things. Meta programs are among the deepest filters of our cognitive world of perceptions and might be classified on several levels of thought.

We are a sensory-based information species, and we process information via our sensory channels of thought. To synchronize ourselves with others, it is important to discover people's preferred re-presentational systems. We have all our preferences about pretty much everything. Conceptually, we delete, distort, generalize, and even adjust our beliefs.

Eye accessing cues are important as is carefully noticing the predicates (verbs, adverbs, adjectives) a person uses when speaking to calibrate the preferred method of being in sync with their world. Visual people sort information by seeing and using lots of visual predicates; auditory people sort information by hearing and using auditory predicates; kinesthetic people usually gesture quite a lot and use "feeling" predicates and prefer to feel things.

To this regard, it is important to present information into the corresponding sensory channel and match the person strategy by juicing up your presentation with the correct meaningful ingredients, creating states of mind and leveraging synchronization.

As human beings, we are a dynamic species, and everything changes all the time. Nothing is static; everything is dynamic in its nature, and some people have the tendency to evaluate events from very different perspectives depending on what the experience means to them.

Some people:

- Gather information through senses, while others appeal to their inner knowledge. Sensors think of themselves as practical and real while they see others as unrealistic and impractical. On the other hand, intuitors trust their intuition. The former use sensory-specific terms and are specifically detailed, whereas the latter communicate with more abstracted views.

- Are judgers. They are more pragmatic, organized, and resolute in comparison to *perceivers* who live their lives and prefer to keep their options open.

- Are more likely to prefer the company of others and are outgoing, needing encouragement from others in order to be socially adept. On the contrary, other people are more introverted and prefer to be alone (not around people) and are more interested in intrapersonal communication, turning their attention inward.

- Scale information related to size [Trees (details) versus forest (global picture)]. Some are deductive (thinkers) and begin with the global picture in mind and then move to specifics. Others (inductive thinkers) start with specific details then move up.

- Have a poetic mindset and reason through storytelling and metaphors.
- Look for sameness and correlation, others for differences.
- Are conservative and love things as they are. Others love change.
- Are interested in finding the reason why things are the way they are, whereas others are focused on solutions and on what to do and how to solve things.
- Favor qualitative over quantitative (specific, factual, numbers, order, measurements) information, and others prefer relating to meaning and to the quality of their experience.
- Think and process information quickly. Others need to take their time to consider things in a thoughtful way and handle information slowly.
- Are quick to change their minds. Others are cautious decision-makers.
- Are focused on costs.
- Are focused on quality.
- Are focused on quantity.
- Et cetera.

Who said that there is nothing rational about the way people decide to buy?

BUYER PERSONA

The very first step is to know your audience. To be successful, you need to analyze your public and study individuals, group formations, loyalties, and relationships within the audience you want to reach. The digital wisdom says you need to focus on creating archetypal and distinct groups of ideal and potential customers. Basically, this is a profiling task—a fundamental, initial step.

Depending on your desired outcome, you need to know everything you can possibly know about your audience:

- Demographic information
- What are their problems, unique challenges, goals, desires?
- How do they communicate?
- How and where do they spend their time?
- What about their friends and families?
- What do they find pleasurable? (and what are their pain points?)
- What do they value most/less? What are their goals?
- How do they do their research? How do they consume information?
- What are their meta programs?
- What are their most common objections to the product or service you are trying to sell?
- How can you help them?
- Can you deliver on your promises?
- What do they expect from you?
- What do they really want?
- What do they consider meaningful?
- How do they construct meaning?
- What do you mean to them?
- How can you create meaning for them?

Once you were able to identify your buyer personas, you can start tailoring and crafting your PRopaganda to inject them with meaning and hypnotize their intent.

*"The analyst of public opinion must begin then by
recognizing the triangular relationship between the scene
of action, the human picture of that scene and
the human response to that picture working itself out
upon the scene of action."*

(WALTER LIPPMANN)

QUACK, QUACK, QUACK... LIKE A DUCK

People have the wrong picture in mind with regard
to hypnosis. There are a lot of stereotypes about this
mysterious art. One is that hypnosis makes people perform
despicable acts. Human beings have always been fascinated
by the power of the mind. Healing techniques that could
resemble hypnosis go back more than 3000 years in time.
Temples of sleep, the power to cure by touch, magnetism,
and a vast range of exotic techniques were used all around
the globe.

The term *hypnosis* is ascribed to Scottish physician James
Braid who came up with the word *hypnotism,* named for the
Greek God Hypnos, the God of Sleep, to describe the process. Hypnosis does not involve sleep, and this association
was absolutely not accurate; it is not even a somnambulistic
state, but the name had stuck.

The inducing of a trance state and the power of suggestion is now proven. The nature of hypnosis is intimately
linked with the subtle relationship between different states
of mind. Everything is hypnosis, and it is argued that people keep moving from one trance to another.

*"Men are so simple of Mind, and so much dominated by
their immediate needs, that a deceitful man will always
find plenty who are ready to be deceived."*

(NICCOLÒ MACHIAVELLI)

SHINE A TORCH

The conscious and the unconscious are not distinct entities;
they are both present at the same time. However, we find it
easy to explain these phenomena by imagining our minds
as an iceberg where the conscious mind is the little part
emerging from the water. Another way of drawing a similar
picture is imagining a darkened room; if you shine a torch,
you will illuminate certain details (conscious), not the unlit
ones (unconscious).

The oldest and emotionally driven part of the brain is
the decision-maker, and the conscious mind justifies behaviors and decisions in a logical fashion that makes sense.
People do things and then come up with reasons that better justify and fit the circumstances. As Martin wrote, *"Only
a part of our mental processes are ever directly finding expression
in our conscious acts and words. The unchosen and the illogical
run along with the desired and the logical material, only we have
learned not to pay attention to such things."* Think of it as a spi-
der being the conscious, moving all around a big web made
of meanings.

The two entities are not separated, and often the
unconscious emerges by sending us signals. The non-con-
scious mind is a stimulus-response mechanism. It adapts to
whatever it's fed and attempts to avoid fear and pain. Many
people fear change because the unconscious tends to avoid
the unknown. Instead, the conscious part possesses critical

faculties. It analyzes and criticizes, and it is the logical part that, sometimes, becomes a barrier to communication.

The father of modern hypnosis, Milton Erickson, developed a new approach to induce hypnotic states (induction) by speaking with the unconscious. He came up with several indirect methods called *permissive techniques*. These techniques are subtle and non-obvious approaches, if compared to authoritarian techniques as a general means. Ordinary conversation gradually starts using language designed to guide people into a trance with some induction technique, such as walking down the stairs of the mind or focusing on a third eye. The induction aims to confuse and bewilder the conscious mind in an attempt to speak directly with the subconscious. This is done to confuse and distract, seeing that a distracted mind is easier to manipulate. No wonder we live in a modern world dominated by infobesity and distractions.

The unconscious mind responds less to well-formed grammar and complete sentences but rather to imagination and moods evoked by key words and phrases. Clearly, liking and rapport are vital for belief and trust.

Belief and trust are critical to hypnosis.

HYPNOTIC LANGUAGE

The brain is a pattern-seeking machine.

One of the main traits of hypnotic language is its purposeful vagueness. When using artfully vague language, the listener is obliged to fill the information voids, to fill the blanks by applying meaning to the words as relevant to his own experience and style of thinking. Vagueness permits to take the message and to attach the meaning that fits one's own needs.

Hypnotic language reduces the specific details in the external world into a select few categories of generalities. The listener then converts the large capacity of general words into specific meanings within his/her own mind.

According to experts John Burton and Bob Bodenhamer, there are three factors, or facets, that allow the mind to be susceptible to language patterns and perceptual principles that affect hypnotic language. These factors are the conscious/unconscious mind split, the specific cognitive style of processing information, and the perceptual principles of Gestalt.

Eating a culinary masterpiece, getting a massage from masseuse, listening to that classical melody that you love, admiring a beautiful painting that drew your attention at the museum, and enjoying a nice glass of wine all induce a trance state and are related to our preferred sensory modalities. Some sort of meaning arises. The kinesthetic buyer wants to feel the softness of the fabric of the dress on her skin, the visual buyer wants to see the product, and the auditory buyer wants to hear some additional information from you.

Hypnotic language presupposes a conscious mind and a rich, resource-filled unconscious mind. The former is limited in its thinking ability, whereas the latter is not. Either our primary (conscious) or secondary (unconscious) awareness consist of all the meanings we have built up through our lives.

As human beings, we have limited capacity to process complex information. Either limited beliefs or frames of mind develop out of our limited cognitive capacity. A master of style knows the conscious focus on words and content and that when content exceeds the processing ability of the primary awareness, it passes to the secondary, the unconscious. For this particular reason, any assertion or statement or question that requires a person to go inside to respond or to answer induces a mild trance state.

In addition to cognitive elements that make the brain conductive to hypnotic language, several principles of human perception play a role in leveraging effectiveness in changing perceptions (e.g. *Perceptual filters*). One of the key factors that plays a role in giving hypnosis this kind of effectiveness is our innate need to organize what we sense in such a ways that allow us to understand information and content. We tend to usually try to organize any stimuli we sense, and how we organize these inputs offers a predictable and patterned avenue for hypnotic language to travel directly to its target, the unconscious mind.

Each day, countless stimuli bombard us. Our sensing provides general information to the brain. We perceive, we think, and we feel. We think and feel about our thinking and feelings. We create meaning and we think about the meanings we create. This is the ultimate meaning-making to our mind-body system.

Basically, we are a perfectly interconnected system network of constant processing, storage, and use of information, and our organizational drive provides the meanings we create through our perceptions.

As Burton and Bodenhamer argue, "*In addition to the cognitive elements that make the brain conductive to hypnotic language, several principles of human perception play a role in making hypnotic language effective in changing perception*":

Figure Ground: The figure-ground principle plays a crucial role in focusing awareness on any group of stimuli that get divided into either figure or ground. By writing about real space and time, Walter Lippmann referred to the "*lost perspective and the background and the dimension of action [that] are clipped and frozen in a stereotype.*" Whatever we pay attention to, we always find more, depending on our filtering mental processes.

Likeness or Similarity: As a shortcut of ours, we sort stimuli and form general categories. In other words, we tend to interpret these stimuli in what we believe to be the most simplistic form to gain a better understanding. Some words or terms possess elastic properties and stretch to cover more than one meaning (e.g. homonyms). By providing multiple meanings for the same piece of information, you have the opportunity to invite the listener to direct his thoughts somewhere else.

Closure: Humans tend to fill in missing pieces in their perceptions. It's the information void we try to fill in with the meaning that best fits our reality in order to close the felt dissonance. We fill in the holes to have wholes. For example, try to say something to someone and pause without finishing your sentence. Your interlocutor will do the job for you.

Simplicity: This suggests that a person sensing a stimulus will draw upon the simplest explanation or perception for the stimulus or collection of stimuli. In part, simplicity means that we tend to interpret in accordance to pre-existing beliefs. (Hypnotic language is said to reduce/override simplicity since it transports the listener from conscious to unconscious mind.) This is perfectly in line with persuasive communication. If you craft your message around the pre-existing beliefs of your audience, you cannot not win their approval.

Dissonance reduction: Dissonance equals internal discomfort and frustration. Knowing the process style of the audience brain enables the communicator to utilize this dynamic in more effective ways, increasing the likelihood of reaching the desired outcome. When a word does not fit the context of the message, the receiver must go inside and search within to examine all the possible meaning choices. Hypnotic communication breaks the traditional rules by setting up the stage for obtaining a sure response from the listener, and unconventional messages force the listener to go into a mild trance in order to search for meaning and understand it.

Continuation: Continuation refers to a person's habitual tendency to group stimuli in a way that minimizes disruptions, and it is similar to the principle of generalizing because we use the same strategy for any situation that we find similar to the point of origin.

In order to process information, the listener must consider the content of the message. Complex concepts must be translated into words and symbols of great significance. Being careful about the content and the context is a prerequisite for creating attention and awareness and intentionally directing thoughts toward a desired outcome.

Messages shall be engineered in substance and form to rouse the desired reply.

"Considertheselettersruntogether."

"Now you felt compelled to decode the letters in the previous collection, didn't you? You just can't help it. And you went into a light trance to do this decoding…"

(JOHN BURTON AND BOB G. BODENHAMER)

THE MILTON MODEL

As a result of many charlatans and misleading information on the subject, there is a lot of confusion on what hypnosis and trance are. Hypnosis is a natural process. We're in a trance when we watch a movie, focus on writing, study, or passionately concentrate on some task, going inward to search for meaning or reflecting deeply. We go from one state to another all the time. All the time.

We are systematic in our language, and the hypnotic language functions as all language does. After having modeled Virginia Satir and Fritz Perls, the NLP cofounders were introduced to Milton Erickson, an American psychiatrist who specialized in hypnosis and therapy, and wrote two volumes on the patterns of hypnotic techniques he used with his clients having developed a powerful set of techniques to access and communicate directly with the unconscious.

Some say that the Milton Model mirrors, in reverse, the original NLP Meta Model. To a certain degree, this might be true, seeing that, essentially, the Meta Model is intentionally very specific to recover deletions, generalizations, and distortions, whereas the Milton Model is artfully vague and metaphoric, asking for the need to chunk up and make new deletions, new generalizations, and new distortions.

However, there is much more to this. NLP adopted the simple logical level system as it distinguished surface versus deep structure statements. As a preliminary remark, it is important to make a distinction between the surface and deep structures. In the 1950s, Noam Chomsky developed his model of linguistics by arguing that each sentence in a language has two levels of representation, a surface structure (written language/actual sounds) and a deep structure (actual meaning of a sentence designed to capture the essence and understanding through intuition and semantics). The Transformational Grammar premise is that if you change wordings, you alter feelings and states of mind.

As language patterns, one shall use a combination of words and phrases that are pre-calculated to capture the imagination of the reader or listener and generate emotional states. The key lies in being able to leverage imagination and create states of mind in other people. As human beings, we have multiple levels of understanding and perception and of meanings. We are stereotyped and we cannot do anything but create images and meanings in our minds. By being sensitive to other people's models of the world, one is able to match the individual subjective experience with the use of words and body language. All of this can activate the unconscious inward mind-search for others to create the meaning you desire inside their heads.

Artfully vague language gives people room to fill in the information blanks. The use of ambiguous words and phrases and vague language leads to mild distractions and trance. As a consequence, the listener is obliged to fill in the voids by applying meaning relevant to his or her own experience and style of thinking.

As Milton Erickson wrote, "*It is time to recognize that meaningful communication should replace repetitious verbigerations, direct suggestions and authoritarian commands.*" In simplistic terms, the goal is to occupy the conscious mind to engage directly with the unconscious part by using language patterns that indirectly move the listener to higher levels of abstract and introspective thinking.

"When I wanted to know something, I wanted it undistorted by somebody else's imperfect knowledge."

(Milton H. Erickson)

THE INVERSE META MODEL

The following is just an example of Bandler and Grinder's findings. It is absolutely not exhaustive and only for the purpose of gaining an overall understanding. Further readings in all these disciplines are presented in the bibliography section for the interested reader.

Mind Reading

Claiming to know thoughts, feelings, motives, or intentions in someone's mind without specifying any process on how you acquired the information:

- I know my boss does not care...
- I perfectly know how you feel... You must be thinking that...
- He knows better than you...
- I know what you are doing... You really are beginning to learn...

By carefully employing this pattern, you can pace and lead people.

Lost Performative

Value judgments that highlight important values but omit identifying the person doing the judging. Politicians use this extensively:

- The Swiss people do not want to...
- American people...
- Australian people...
- Europeans...

These are broad generalizations deleting everyone that does not agree with the statement made. [Example: We carry the finest global women's brands in the world. (Message: You are purchasing the best)]

Cause and Effect

Are statements implying that a particular action causes a specific reaction. X causes Y is a strong form of linguistic linkage:

- The simplest example could be: you make me crazy.
- You make me feel ___
- I made this mistake because of you
- You will understand as soon as you read this

This implies that if you do X, Y will materialize.

Complex Equivalence

Suggests that one thing is related to and means something else (it may or may not be true), utilizing words of equation:

- She is late. That must mean that she went to bed late yesterday night.
- You got the degree. You must be clever.
- This suit is the best. It is made for you.

It is fundamentally using a part of our experience (external behavior) to be equivalent to our meaning making (internal state)by linking things together, confusing map and territory and directing the listener to create new maps for navigating his/her matrix.

Presuppositions

Conceptual and linguistic assumptions. Something that is unstated but, at the same time, assumed to be present (true).

The listener must use clauses of predicates for the statement to understand and make sense of the communication.

These might be temporal with words suggesting the passage/importance of time (when, often, before, during, while) or ordinal by sequencing the listener's experience and using numbers and positions.

As Bandler and Grinder wrote, *"Message A is a presupposition of message B when message A must be a true statement necessary for message B and the message not B.'*

Universal Quantifiers

Universal generalizations that imply absoluteness. The category represents the whole group, and there are no exceptions to the current experience.

- All marketers are liars.
- Everybody knows.
- Everyone working for the Public Admin is lazy.

This implies absolute conditions as being true.

Modal Operators of Necessity/Possibility

It is our Modus Operandi (MO)—style of operation. MO of necessity suggests that something is required or not required to happen (words that suggest something is necessary or possible).

Necessity (must/must not, should/should not, have or need to...)

- You should learn... versus You shouldn't learn...
- You really need to adapt to a brand new mindset...

Possibility (can/cannot, possible/impossible, am/am not...)

- I cannot...
- You can...
- It's possible to change your attitude.

These Modal Operators define our model of the world and provide useful linguistic structures.

Nominalizations

Nominalizations refer to processes represented as things (verbs turned into nouns). We live in a process world and nouns are static whereas verbs are dynamic.

As human beings, we love to simplify things and do not like confusion. As a consequence, we turn processes into nouns (to choose becomes choice, to communicate becomes communication, to decide becomes decision, etc.). The key point here is being able to send people inward on a transderivational search for meaning by filling language with nominalizations as if they were static things.

A semantically loaded nominalization works pretty much the same as the unspecified verb by implying action without describing how the action has occurred or will occur. It is vague and by not specifying any action the unspecified verbs maximize the possibility for any statement to fit other people's subjective experience (...wonder...wish... know...learn)—a way to reach a conclusion about something without indicating the process for which you arrive at that conclusion.

Lack of Referential Index

The sentence purposefully fails to specify who is the agent or object of an action. Pronouns are not specified and offer the opportunity to pace the listener.

- Nobody cares!
- They never listen to me.
- One can be hopeless.

Comparative Deletion (Unspecified Comparison)

A comparison that is made without specifying who or what is being compared. It does not include any further criteria:

- You are the best.
- This is the best alternative.

THE MILTON MODEL CATEGORY

Tag questions are questions added/placed at the end of a statement or question to increase compliance. It draws the conscious mind's attention and allows other information to go directly to the unconscious:

- ..... Have you?
- .... Isn't it?
- .... Will you?
- .... Didn't I?
- You can, can you not?

Pace Current Experience

It is the use of sensory-based, grounded, behaviorally specific information to describe the current experience by taking statements that agree with and have similarities to the person's ongoing experience:

- ... as you breathe.
- You hear what I'm saying.
- As you notice external sounds...

This can be added to the utilization of the current experience by incorporating whatever happens and using everything the other person says in the process of communicating, for instance:

- Communicator 1: I don't think I know.
- Communicator 2: That is right, you don't think you know...

Embedded Commands

Are short, hidden suggestions that form part of a larger sentence for the purpose of engaging the listener in a certain train of thought or asking them to take action. These commands are subtly stressed by analogical marking (e.g. with volume, tonality, body language) in order to alert the listener's unconscious of its importance. By stressing the command part with a higher or lower tone of voice or emphasizing specific and concise words with the use of gestures, one speaks to the conscious but, in the meantime, commands something to the unconscious mind of the listener.

Conversational Postulate

A rhetorical question that, if taken literally, would require a response or action. These may include embedded commands to do something.

- Can you *hear what I'm saying* ? (this implies: hear what I'm saying)
- Can you *speak now?* (this implies: speak now)

Basically, they're indirect communication carried as a command but do not sound as such.

Extended Quote

A succession of quotes designed to create mild confusion in the listener, increase suggestibility and compliance, and embed process instructions or commands. They take attention away from you as the speaker and displace the conscious mind so information can travel into the unconscious.

These quotes might refer to something heard from a friend, something seen on television, or something read in a brochure. I particularly like Speed Seduction Master Ross Jeffries' explanation: *"Quotes allow us to test the other person's readiness and her responsiveness to the subject. If we see that she is confused or having a negative response, we step back from it. We say, 'I'd never say anything like that or I think that is silly, stupid.'"*

Ambiguity

Is the artful use of words or statements that have more than one meaning. This leaves the full meaning to the imaginations of the listeners to fit their own realities of the world. Words that are ambiguous in context work pretty well to influence minds.

In this particular case, there might be several deep structures for a single surface structure. This prompts a transderivational search on the part of the listener. As a consequence, commands travel easily to the subconscious (which is overlooked by the busy conscious mind) and lead to a mild trance while trying to sort out the ill-defined meanings.

Phonological (They are written differently but have the same sound):

- *You're/Your*

Syntactic (Syntax ambiguity lacks clarity and one cannot immediately determine the function of the word from the context):

- Running water
- Hypnotizing hypnotists

Punctuation (Prompts confusion with the help of well-formed sentences joined by a word or a phrase to create an ill-formed sentence):

- Improper pauses
- Use of dots (...)
- Incomplete sentences

Scope ambiguity (The context is not clear as to which part of a sentence verbs or modifiers apply. As a result, one does not understand how much one portion of a sentence applies to another):

- I was riding an elephant with my trousers on (you or the elephant?)
- Use of words that presuppose the listener to accept the quality of everything that follows, such as *kindly, usefully, surprisingly...*
- Presupposing truth by the use of words, such as *realize, know, become aware of, understand,* or attributing intelligence or feelings to inanimate objects.

METAPHORS CAN BE ANYTHING

A joke, a sentence, a little story, or a quote from mythology.

The referent used here is the content versus context, and the message is embedded within an unrelated story, which offers the possibility to bypass the listener's conscious awareness. As we saw in reference to hypnotic language patterns, Burton and Bodenhamer found that three specific factors allow minds to be susceptible to hypnotic language: the conscious and unconscious mind, the cognitive style of processing information, and perceptual principles of Gestalt.

Stories, metaphors, and fairy tales influence minds and permit the hidden message to travel to the unconscious and influence the processing of information. With metaphors, certain aspects or factors are highlighted by analogies and provide the structure for making sense of irrelevant, yet ambiguous, information.

The identical movie, story, or fairy tale is never the same for all of us. It depends on our subjective experience. No two experiences are alike in the whole world when it comes to our unique being. Everything is interpreted in a different way, and people have the tendency to identify themselves in the character of a book or a movie at a very sympathetic and empathic level. We must remember that anything in the world can be associated with and compared to everything else. In order to influence the individual, it is categorically imperative to keep in mind these ideas.

It does not really depend on the original thinking or idea. Everything might become a common bond regardless of its origins.

The Butterfly Effect might lead to the same destination.

"Excellence then, is not an act, but a habit."

(ARISTOTLE)

COVERT COMMUNICATION

The human organism is made of interconnected learning systems. We are learners. We learn languages and behaviors. We learn bad and good habits. We learn by repetition.

Seeing that we are extremely lazy, we create habits and shortcuts and then become very good at not changing them. Throughout our entire lifespan, our mind is conditioned by experiences and learned stereotypes that easily lead a stimulus-response patterned mechanism. By somatizing, we translate patterns into every little cell of our mind-body system. These habits might be found in our unconscious mind along with many other important functions and skills.

Network science is a field of study that combines computer science with Network and Graph theory and examines the principles that govern network behaviors. Networks are constantly interrelated, and there is a constant input, exchange, processing, storage, and output of information. Behaviors are dynamic in their essence and change all the time. Our unconscious mind is always alert, and it picks up the sending and receiving of verbal and nonverbal communication without us even being aware of it. For this particular reason, if you want to intentionally manipulate someone else's states of mind, you need to avoid awaking the conscious part by significant questioning. To avoid or reduce such, the critical conscious thought must be bypassed in a disguised and subtle way, without the process being known to the listener. To alter behaviors, you must influence the unconscious and not reason with the conscious part of people's minds.

Behaviors might be altered by dictated activities or by altering the external behavior, surroundings, and environments, but this is likely to lead to some resistance. Nothing in the world is forever static and everything can be changed from internal states to attitudes, opinions, processes, emotions, and feelings.

Perceptions, perspectives, and stereotypes can be manufactured and result in closing the loop by changing behaviors. How well you carefully frame your message can alter judgments and results.

Mental shifts and reframing invite a change in perspective toward any desired outcome.

REFRAMING MEANING

Arguing on the historical context of perceptions, some say that there is no meaning without context. Even W. Shakespeare, in *Hamlet*, wrote, *"There is nothing either good or bad, but thinking makes it so."* Quoted by Bandler and Grinder, a very old Chinese Taoist story*"describes a farmer in a poor country village. He was considered very well-to-do, because he owned a horse which he used for plowing and for transportation. One day his horse ran away. All his neighbors exclaimed how terrible* *this was, but the farmer simply said...Maybe. A few days later the horse returned and brought two wild horses with it. The neighbors all rejoiced at his good fortune, but the farmer just said...Maybe. The next day the farmer's son tried to ride one of the wild horses; the horse threw him and broke his leg. The neighbors all offered their sympathy for his misfortune, but the farmer again said... Maybe. The next week conscription officers came to the village to take young men for the army. They rejected the farmer's son because of his broken leg. When the neighbors told him how lucky he was, the farmer replied...Maybe."*

Words and symbols are very powerful. With extremely flexible syntax and the use of images, we can induce states of mind. We can alter minds and transform carefully crafted meaning. Just think about prolific American inventor Thomas A. Edison and the light bulb. When he was attacked by people saying he failed many times, he simply replied that he did not consider it a failure. He just discovered a thousand ways not to make a lamp. Different frame, different perception. He reframed horizontally by shifting the semantics to a totally different perspective—a new meaning.

The different framing or perspective of anything has the power to shift thinking in a dramatic fashion. Over our lifespans, we have built up our own beliefs and our own maps for navigating the world, and we are full of stereotypes. Some are useful, whereas sometimes we've built up sabotaging thoughts by inventing erroneous conclusions. Often, we are so convinced that things are how we personally perceive them that we do not even acknowledge other people's points of view. This is a great conversational and cognitive mistake. At the end, it is all about thoughts. Thoughts make up beliefs and thoughts might be redirected to a new perspective in order to directionalize one's consciousness.

We do it all the time. We wrap up frames around our thoughts, events, situations, and the like. We make up our internal realities, and our belief constructions govern our conceptual reasoning.

Hall and Bodenhamer highlight that everything begins with our thoughts. All means nothing. Meaning has no meaning in the real world. We invent meaning. We are meaning-makers by nature. The key to comprehending these phenomena is to realize that meaning does not really exist in the world. We invent everything from meaning to beliefs. Meaning arises from our thinking, and it lies in the evaluative understanding of each of us. Beliefs arise and solidify from our thinking as well. When we validate our thoughts, we create beliefs.

We create frames of reference. We construct beliefs and our conceptual world of meaning. By cognitively restructuring our perspectives and our frames of reference, we can change our beliefs and create new meanings. We can modify our perception of the world.

How we frame meaning influences cognitive responses. It is all about perceptions and meaning.

"If the doors of perception were cleansed, everything would appear as it is—infinite."

(WILLIAM BLAKE)

JUST SAY YES! NOW!

Logically, rewording or repricing a product or service does not add any value to it. Emotionally it does and sometimes we find ourselves giving mindless, patterned responses to words and symbols.

Yes and *No* are two powerful words that express either affirmatives or negatives. More often than not, we are eager for others to say *yes* to our requests. This is particularly true in the sales field but can be easily applied to any situation in our everyday lives. We are selfish and we are egoists, aren't we?

Academics and professionals have done all sorts of research to discover how it is possible to change minds—to influence and persuade other people to our thinking in order to gain compliance—and discovered many magical words that have a strong impact in getting people to respond in a positive way to our requests—to *open sesame*.

For instance, the word *because* is related to the philosophical concept of causality, a strong cause-effect trigger. Harvard social psychologist Ellen J. Langer did an experiment to demonstrate that people like to have a reason to back up their behavior. The experiment consisted of people waiting in line to use a library copy machine and experimenters asking to get ahead in line with an excuse:

- "Excuse me, I have five pages. May I use the Xerox machine because I'm in a rush?"
- "Excuse me, I have five pages. May I use the Xerox machine?"
- "Excuse me, I have five pages. May I use the Xerox machine because I have to make some copies?"

The results of the experiment demonstrated that the reason was not a matter of the excuse itself. People said *yes* simply due to the word *because*. It is noteworthy to mention that almost all of us have been preprogrammed to this particular word since we were kids and then teenagers. Remember when we asked our parents if we could go to that nice party everyone was attending? The answer: *No*. And if you were to ask for reasons: "***Because I said so.***"

The same principle, as explained by social psychology experts Cialdini and Hogan, goes for the word *now*. This word is wrapped with authority and not negotiable since childhood:

"Dad, can I go out with friends?"

*"Nope, go to bed. **Now**!"*

Most marketing and sales techniques utilize the "Buy **Now**" technique, either emphasizing authority and, sometimes, the law of scarcity. Another great word is imagine; by using it we are sending out our message without being afraid of any resistance from the counterparty. In fact, we are not telling others what to do. Instead, we create images in their minds by asking them to **just** *imagine...*

Furthermore, we do not have to undervalue the power of kindness. By asking things in a kind way and thanking people, we are gaining top scores within the communication magic sphere (***please, thank you***).

The fashionable devil's ***control*** and ***fear*** wordings can also have a powerful impact on people's minds. In the end, we all want to feel in control of our lives, and each of us is sensible to dangerous situations (either real or imagined). Just think about life insurance reps who try their best to make you feel in control whilst leveraging your deepest fears in order to close a sale or the fashionable devil herself who leverages your fears to be in control.

Another important aspect is found in names. We like people who remember our names. We hate people who get our name wrong or refer to us as "Dear Customer,..." (I am not a number or a target, I am XY!).

It is argued that the use of people's names enlarges our chances to succeed in the sales arena and in life. Just be careful, do not use a name too much, and, most importantly, do not ever get the name wrong.

"I have been a believer in the magic of language since, at a very early age, I discovered that some words got me into trouble and others got me out."

(KATHERINE DUNN)

WORDS ARE STEREOTYPED POWER

Words are magic, aren't they?

Lippmann said, "*In some measure, stimuli from the outside, especially when they are printed or spoken words, evoke some part of a system of stereotypes, so that the actual sensation and the preconception occupy consciousness at the same time. The two are blended, much as we looked at red through blue glasses and saw green. If what we are looking at corresponds successfully with what we anticipated, the stereotype is reinforced for the future.*" Emotionally loaded words have a great power over people. A single word evokes images that are more detailed than any possible description. What comes to your mind reading the following?

- WAR
- TRAGEDY
- LOVE
- PEACE
- WIN
- WORK
- SEX
- FUN
- KILL
- HEAVEN
- GOD

- EXPERIENCE
- FAITH

They have a heavy semantic weight, don't they? They're simple yet powerful words because of our stereotyped mindset. Words can injure and wound or get you well. They are magic and they are a powerful weapon to either seduce minds or repel them.

Language affects our entire neuro-semantic system made up of beliefs, emotions, perceptions, and values. Just as appearance, language must be appropriate to the setting. You do not speak in the same way at a classic concert as you do at a footy match.

The careful choice of words, tonality, and grammar articulation and style is a masterful art. In the whole world, there are few people who are truly masters of style. On the other hand, it all depends on the audience and the context, and it has to be noted that advanced and eloquent structures might be very nice, but if your public struggles to comprehend and make sense of the complex sentences you are propagating, they will surely think you are clever and well educated, but your message will not travel anywhere. The clarity of the message leads to clarity of comprehension and makes it easier for you to persuade minds.

Another main problem lies in the fact that many words are overused. This is what marketing star David Meerman Scott calls "*Gobbledygook phrases and wording.*" They have been (ab)used so much that they have completely lost their competitive appeal.

Language is a fantastic tool. We have the opportunity to play with words and with content. We can package and reframe meanings or even create new meanings and change perspectives and perceptions. Take failing for example. In our Westernized society, not passing an exam equals failure, which semantically implies that you are a total failure.

Isn't it better to consider it as feedback to get better next time? We were not born geniuses; we learn and we cannot be stopped by a word, can we?

In the online and offline world, word choice is absolutely critical. It is well-proven that words affect our neurology and shall be chosen with meticulous care, keeping in mind that sometimes no words are a better alternative than too many words. Unless the intention is to trigger negative feelings or to apply negative weight to your message (as in war PRopaganda), it is strongly suggested to use positive words.

Good articulation shows competence and credibility. Speaking your audience's lingo and adjusting your everyday language to your buyers' personas in a personal and human way is critical (avoid nasty tech lingo that no one understands).

The right words elicit states of mind and the use of a full set of sensory intelligence and details might stimulate minds by evoking strong emotional connotations. Remember to acknowledge other points of view and never say that others are wrong; it would be pretentious and lead to defensive behavior—trouble.

Keep it simple and paint vivid pictures in your prospects' minds by wearing the shoes of the Michelangelo of language.

Color minds with vivid images.

"It would not be impossible to prove with sufficient repetition and psychological understanding of the people concerned that a square is in fact a circle. What after all are a square and a circle? They are mere words and words can be molded until they clothe ideas in disguise."

(JOSEPH GOEBBELS)

A WORLD OF SYMBOLISM

Symbols are a visual and extremely vivid simplification of more complex conceptual issues. Their purpose is to convey meaning, and their emotional impact is very strong on minds.

In 1956, Noam Chomsky created the Transformational Grammar model and argued that we are wired to construct meanings and to hold representations constant as we invent a world of meaning within our minds.

We are born with a language acquisition device that programs us for language readiness, and this is how we enter the symbolic dimension; we work with symbols in order to live in the symbolic world of language and abstractions. There are multiple levels of meanings that make up the psychic context of the human mind and govern it. Everything is influenced by meaning.

The Bible says, "*You shall not make for yourself a carved image, or any likeness of anything that is in heaven above, or that is in the earth beneath, or that is in the water under the earth*" but, as human beings, we cannot do without symbols.

Devotion to flags, statues, wooden idols, and images, is seductive and powerful to leveraging our emotional states. In line with Lippmann's reasoning, "*Symbols are often so useful and so mysteriously powerful that the word itself exhales a magical glamour. In thinking about symbols it is tempting to treat them as if they possessed independent energy. The museums and books of folklore are full of dead emblems and incantations, since there is no power in the symbol, except that which it acquires by association in the human mind.*" This is the seduction of the subjective experiences people feel by manipulating their stereotyped thinking—the seduction of illusions. Symbols connect and are the translation and embodiment of ideologies, concepts, opinions, and even people associated with them.

Symbols have been extremely important to human beings since antiquity. Visual spectacles may have a striking effect on the mind.

Just think of the Swastika.

It was an ancient symbol widely used in many cultures. It meant good fortune and good luck.

That is true no longer.

THE MEANINGFUL PROPAGANDA OF MEANING

We are semantic and symbolic creatures made up of complex psychic and neurological layers that are embedded within layers that are embedded within yet more complex layers. The Semantic Web Layer Cake is by no means as complex as our brains.

Motivational drives are instinct-like impulses in their nature and become needs or desires as we attribute meaning to them. It all begins with a neutral state of awareness. The stimulus-response formula is our hyperlinked foundation of more complex meaning-making powers. We have some innate drives (food, air, water, sex) to survive, whereas everything else is learned. Some patterns might habituate and become normalcy. Everything else is created by our faculty of making meaning via several processes of thinking, reasoning, associating, evaluating, framing, and labeling.

Thinking constructs meaning and, as Protagoras said, *"Man is the measure of all things."* It all starts at a cognitive level and soon becomes somatic and affects our feelings. We are joyful and we see the rainbow in an ever-sunny world. We are fearful or angry and our flee/fight responses fire off in an instant.

In this era of chaos, we need to be informed on how we operate and how others create their maps of the world. This is an important aspect of our worlds (business, culture, education). A curious and fluid mind is needed. Exploring, questioning, and establishing better communication and understanding are keys to better living and to a better society, to better relationships, and to new and better meanings for a better world.

We need to respectfully recognize that each of us is different. This does not have anything to do with the color of our skin or our religious faith. We are unique. As a symbolic and semantic class of life, we thrive on ideas; we thrive on meaning and we move forward by interpreting things and creating new meanings.

Via thought we create meaning. We input data and process information, we make up our realities, and we can change meanings seeing that meaning does not really possess any external existence. Meaning is a creation of ours and might change multiple times a day; its fluidity and plasticity are context-sensitive. Meaning is conveyed through the channels of thought. In today's e-market, people thrive on ideas, meaning, and purpose.

Everything in the world asks for meaning. Without it we'd go nowhere.

People are full of needs. Intentional meanings influence people's perceptual filters and help us to construct the reasons for which they want something. Their intentions are moved forward by what they believe as being valuable. What people intend to do arises and relies upon the meaning they attach to things they deem important.

Earning attention is no longer enough. It is not about your product and service. It is not about technology advancements. It is not about robots and web-based tech. It is all about people. It is all about creating meaning for them.

Wrap yourself, your product or service, and your company around compelling meaning. Create states, tell semantically loaded stories worth buying, and make people feel good about themselves when they are around you by creating a world to which people want to belong.

Intentionally propagate quality meanings and purpose to stir ultimate passion.

ATTENTION IS NOT ENOUGH

Attention means awareness.

In today's complex world, earning attention is fundamental as a first step in the process leading to the desired outcome: intention. Intention comes after attention; it is something that happens inside ourselves.

We create our own realities—our maps of the world and matrices. We create our meanings. Meaning begins at the primary level of attention and awareness when we simply link, associate, compare, and contrast things. We upload information in the form of words, symbols, happenings, images, videos, posts, and the like. We paint images inside our heads, and we may even install the same in other people, directing and channeling their thoughts.

Inside our minds, we loop around and process all the inputs by creating new meanings about the meanings we have previously created and attached to the objects of our awareness. Typically, what comes to mind is a re-presentation of something that caught our attention; however, before we make a choice of path motivating and orienting us to make some sort of decision or go in a certain direction, we rely on intention, based on meaning, choice, and what's socially acceptable.

If you want to communicate effectively and persuasively, you need to create and provide the quality of meanings that promote a deeper educational understanding in other people's brains. Unless you are able to control every source of information, you cannot have total control of your PRopaganda, and you need to make it easy for people to connect among themselves to share your Gospel by architecting their decision-making processes and thinking.

Intention and meaning are found at a deeper level of our minds if compared to attention and awareness—a higher level where motivation, wants, and desires reside.

To be the Michelangelo of the mind, you shall rise to higher levels than primary awareness.

PROVOKING CREDIBILITY

Fundamentally, credibility is the ability to be perceived as such. People see you as an authoritative source and are then willing to listen to you, believe what you say, and trust you.

Thought-provoking, cool, entertaining, educational, and persistent efforts are great traits if compared to the boring and me-too follower style, aren't they?

The basic rule is to keep your message smooth, short, easy, and simple and to promote positive meaning through your PRopaganda to direct and channel thoughts that are in line with your desired course of action.

Repeat.

Make it easy for people to understand, share, and spread the word.

IT'S ALL ABOUT MEANING

We all interpret anything as we happen to understand it.

Information in—energy out, as explained by Hall, *"describes the heart of meaning-making in our mind-body system. As we input data, we process that data as information. Then we continue to process it up all the levels of the mind. We process data as beliefs, decisions, values and identities. Then we output that information as we 'metabolize' our layers of thoughts and beliefs into energy, as emotional energy, somatic energy, and eventually as the energy of speech and behavior that outwardly expresses our meanings."*

Don't be distracted by the outer shape of reality; meaning is created and you should always seek inner meanings. There are multiple levels of meaning that might create and fire semantic triggers and reactions. Meaning is the most critical and powerful element on the entire planet.

One shall be able to create and project credible meanings for others by repainting images in their minds by offering direction of thought, attribution of meaning, and purpose and by seducing intention. It is creating, assisting, educating, and helping others create their realities of the world in line with your objectives.

This is much more than mirroring or matching stereotyped and associative behaviors through words, body language, and representations. This means discovering people's true motives, purpose, and agenda and being able to intentionally propagate quality meanings to help them to translate their hopes and dreams into intentional action.

Our primary awareness is conditioned by meaning and by association and contrast, whereas our self-reflexive nature brings us into a conceptual world of ideas, values, concepts, and abstract understandings. Being meaning-makers, we attribute meanings to pretty much everything and we create other meanings—meanings upon meanings. The sole purpose of earning attention is not enough because people reflect on their awareness and think about their thinking and feelings and make up layers of meanings inside their heads over the primary attention-meaning encounter.

Awareness is the very first step for others to map their subjective experience of the world and to construct their meanings to abstract levels of thought and consciousness, departing from a process of associating thoughts and feelings all the way to meanings, desires, intentions, and abstract, yet unique, realities.

People learn to give meaning. Hence, you shall educate them by directing their thoughts. Vehicle your Marketing PRopaganda to help people become better decision-makers.

Seize their attention by directionalizing intention.

THE FORMULA OF INFLUENCE

There is no magic wand, but we are patterned and, to a certain degree of accuracy, our behaviors can be predicted. Despite the fact that we are a semantic and symbolic class of life, words and symbols are not perfect vehicles of meanings, but they have the power to evoke and leverage images and feelings in our minds.

We associate, we remember, we map associative meanings, and we create frames of mind that can be exploited by the ones who know how we reason, how we know what we think we know, and how we make decisions. Influence is a contagious process of illusions and new meanings. The illusion of an individual might lead to a process of contagion and to mass suggestion. Everything shall be appropriate to the context. The source, the message itself, and the audience's emotional states all carry the same important weight.

As the source of the message, you must be sensitive to other people's models of the world and prepare the ground to be perceived as credible by your audience. Your audience must perceive you as an authority in your area of expertise in order to trust you. If people trust you, it is much easier for your PRopaganda to travel to their minds without having them argue with its content. Fundamentally, it's all about people's perceptions and being able to arouse their emotional states at the right point in time through the offer of quality meanings.

The world needs clear communication and meaning. Most of the time, trouble comes from misunderstandings, bad communication, or lack of purpose. In life, we need the cooperation of others and we need to become sharper communicators and influencers to get what we want. One might exercise the use of ambiguity, sensory-rich language, quotes, metaphors, or vague language to persuade, overload, and distract the conscious mind and induce confusion. Vagueness, for instance, is extremely important because our brain tends to fill the blanks to create its own meanings that are associated to the meanings we have mapped throughout our lives. It is open to interpretation. The use of vague language might differ depending on intention. Vague language influences, but the listeners might interpret your words in their own way. If you need to attract by laying out a magnetic impression of unshakable principles toward the clear understanding of a concept or idea, it is better to be much clearer and concise.

The most important issue is integrity. In the world we live in, we need to be genuine and do our best to help each other toward a better world where everyone gains. By creating meaning and purpose for other people, you will be able to make others feel good about themselves and about you and influence them to your way of thought.

What's needed is a better understanding of us and other people for a better and more effective communication between humans—a new kind of mindset driven by meaning.

"Be Yourself. Everyone else is already taken."

(OSCAR WILDE)

THE FLAG OF DESTINY

The world is made up of billions of minds connecting and interrelating with other minds. What's in it for people to have anything to do with you? What do you mean to them? Are you the one who makes their worlds a better place, or do you just want to take advantage of their realities?

Taking advantage of and profiting from other people leads to frustration, malcontent, and distrust and it destroys relationships. Knowledge arises from learning and meaning is created by our thinking. Everything results from our holistic meaning-making minds. To influence minds, you need to educate them and direct their thinking processes toward your desired outcome. To master people's motives and drives, you need to create and attribute a rich, robust, and authentic sense of meaningfulness to their meaning-making habits.

The fluid nature of people's consciousness might be resourcefully redirected by adding meaningful value to the process. Conquering awareness and offering quality meanings leads to enhancing other people's quality of life.

Attention and awareness alone might fire off thinking processes and see-hear-feel representations but never reach the conceptual and abstract levels of the mind. To create and shape events that influence minds is a consistent and enduring effort. Repetition is important to keep memory drives, but exceeding expectations due to surprising and supreme meanings is the key to a better future.

The whole basis of successful Marketing PRopaganda is to orchestrate occurrences to appeal to your publics' minds and stir ultimate passions. Whoever can unify and supply people with authentic and sublime meanings easily becomes their master.

Meaning casts hypnotic spells.

Life itself lives on meaning.

> *"But he that dares not grasp the thorn*
> *should never crave the rose."*

(ANNE BRONTË)

Feel free to share with anyone who you believe may find this book meaningful.

THIS IS THE END

The title of this last section is *a bit tricky*. This is not the end because, as Abraham Maslow said, "*There shall be no ultimate satisfaction.*"

I hope that this book was interesting, engaging and entertaining as it was meant to be and all the information in it will be beneficial to you.

Meaning is the most critical element on earth and human beings cannot live without it. To quote Carl Gustav Jung, "*we shall stand against complete atomization into nothingness or meaninglessness. Man cannot stand a meaningless life.*"

The ultimate and necessary condition of life purposes is Meaning.

Thank you for reading.

I wish you all the best meanings,
Francesco
www.francescoferzini.ch

BIBLIOGRAPHY

Here's a partial list of amazing books that I had the pleasure to read or reread while working on this manuscript, and I recommend them to all those interested in the topics discussed. The list of books is less than a bibliography since, over the years, many other experiences contributed to building the worlds of meaning I carry around in my mind. To each author: **Thank you** for having created new and sublime meanings to help others navigate through their worlds of meaning.

Aristotle. *Rhetoric.* Translated by Roberts W. Rhys, 2011. Indo-European Publishing.

Bandler, Richard and John Grinder. *Trance Formations: Neuro-Linguistic Programming and the Structure of Hypnosis,* 2008. Health Communications, USA.

Bandler, Richard. *Usare il Cervello per Cambiare,* 1986. Casa Editrice Astrloabio.

Bandler, Richard and John Grinder. *The Structure of Magic, Vol. 1: A Book About Language and Therapy,* 1975, Science and Behavior Books, Inc.

Bandler, Richard and John Grinder. *Patterns of the Hypnotic Techniques of Milton H. Erickson, M.D., Vol. 1,* 1975, Meta Publications.

Bandler, Richard, et al. *Programmazione NeuroLinguistica*, 1982, Casa Editrice Astrolabio.

Bandler, Richard and John La Valle. *Persuasion Engineering*, 1996. NLP Italy. Alessio Roberti Editore.

Bandler, Richard and Will MacDonald. *Guida per l'esperto alle submodalità*, 1991. Casa Editrice Astrolabio.

Bandler, Richard. *Get the Life You Want: The Secrets to Quick and Lasting Life Change with Neuro-Linguistic Programming*, 2008, Health Communications, Inc.

Barron, David R. and Danek S. Kaus. *Power Persuasion: Using Hypnotic Influence in Life, Love and Business*, 2005. Robert D. Reed Publishers.

Bernays, Edward L. *Propaganda*, 1928. LG Publishing.

Bernays, Edward L. *Crystallizing Public Opinion*, 1923. LG Publishing.

Bernays, Edward L. "The Engineering of Consent," 1947. Journal article.

Borg, James. "Body Language," 2008. Pearson Education Ltd.

Branden, Nathaniel. *Taking Responsibility: Self-Reliance and the Accountable Life*, 1996. NY: Fireside Book, Simon & Schuster.

Burton, John and Bob G. Bodenhamer. *Hypnotic Language*, 2000. Crown House Publishing.

Chomsky, Noam. *Media Control, Second Edition: The Spectacular Achievements of Propaganda*, 2002. Open Media Book.

Chomsky, Noam. *Profit Over People: Neoliberalism & Global Order*, 1999. Seven Stories Press.

Cialdini, Robert B. *Influence: The Psychology of Persuasion*, 1993. Quill William Morrow NY.

Cicero, Tullius M. *De Inventione*, 1949. Cambridge Loeb Classic.

Dilts, Robert. *I Livelli di Pensiero*, NLP Italy. Alessio Roberti Editore.

Dilts, Robert. *Il Potere delle Parole e della PNL*. NLP Italy. Alessio Roberti Editore.

Martin, Everett Dean. *The behavior of crowds: a psychological study*, 1920. Harper & Brothers Publishers: NY and London.

Frankl, Viktor E. *Man's Search for Meaning*, 2006. Beacon Press.

Gellatly, Angus and Oscar Zarate. *Introducing Mind & Brain: A Graphic Guide*, 1999. Totem Books.

Godin, Seth. *Unleashing the Ideavirus*, 2001. Do you Zoom.

Godin, Seth. *Permission Marketing: Turning Strangers Into Friends and Friends Into Customers*, 1999. Simon and Schuster, Inc.

Goodwin, Paul and George Wright. *Decision Analysis for Managing Judgment*, 2009. John Wiley & Sons.

Greene, Robert. *Death and Life of Philosophy*, 1999. St. Augustine's Press, Indiana.

Greene, Robert. *The 48 Laws of of Power*, 2002. Hoodder Books.

Hall, Michael L. *Movie Mind: Directing Your Mental Cinemas*, 2006. Neuro Semantics Publications, USA.

Hall, Michael L. *Meta States: Mastering the High Levels of Your Mind*, 2008. Neuro Semantics Publications, USA.

Hall, Michael L. *Secrets of Personal Mastery*, 2001. Crown House Publishing.

Hall, Michael L. *Games Business Experts Play*, 2002. Crown House Publishing.

Hall, Michael L. *The Matrix Model: The 7 Matrices of Neuro-Semantics*, 2002. Neuro Semantics Publications, USA.

Hall, Michael L. *Winning the Inner Game: Mastering the Inner Game for Peak Performance*, 2007. Neuro Semantics Publications, USA.

Hall, Michael L. *Self-Actualization Psychology: The Psychology of the Bright Side of Human Nature*, 2008. Neuro Semantics Publications, USA.

Hall, Michael L. *Communication Magic*, 2001. Crown House Publishing.

Hall, Michael L. *Secrets of Personal Mastery*, 2000. Crown House Publishing.

Hall, Michael L. *Unleashing Leadership: Self-Actualizing Leaders and Companies*, 2009. Neuro Semantics Publications, USA.

Hall, Michael L. and Bob G. Bodenhamer. *Figuring Out People: Reading People Using Meta-Programs*, 2000. Neuro Semantics Publications, USA.

Hall, Michael L. and Bob G. Bodenhamer. *Mind Lines: Lines for Changing Minds*, 2010. Neuro Semantics Publications, USA.

Hall, Michael L. et al. *The Structure of Personality*, 2003. Crown House Publishing.

Hall, Michale L and Bob G. Bodenhamer. *La Time-Line della PNL*, NLP Today, Alessio Roberti Editore.

Halligan, Brian and Dharmesh Shah. *Inbound Marketing: Get Found Using Google, Social Media, and Blogs (New Rules Social Media Series)*, 2009. John Wiley & Sons.

Herman, Edward S. and Noam Chomsky. *Manufacturing Consent: The Political Economy of the Mass Media*, 2002. Pantheon Books NY.

Hitler, Adolf. *Mein Kampf.* Translated by Michael Ford. Élite Minds, Inc.

Hogan, Kevin. *The Psychology of Persuasion: How to Persuade Others To Your Way of Thinking*, 1996.

Pelican Publishing, Louisiana.

Hogan, Kevin. *The Science of Influence: How to Get Anyone to Say "Yes" in 8 Minutes or Less!*, 2001. John Wiley & Sons

Hogan, Kevin. *Covert Hypnosis 2020: An Operator's Manual*, 2011. Network 3000 Publishing.

Hogan, Kevin. *Covert Persuasion: Psychological Tactics and Tricks to Win the Game*, 2006. John Wiley & Sons.

Hogan, Kevin. Irresistible Attraction: Secrets of Personal Magnetism, 2000. Network 3000 Publishing.

Le Bon, Gustave. *The Crowd: A Study of the Popular Mind*, 2002. Dover Publications, Inc.

Liebermann, David J. *Get Anyone to Do Anything: Never Feel Powerless Again—With Psychological Secrets to Control and Influence Every Situation*, 2000. St. Martin's Griffin, NY.

Lippmann, Walter. *Public Opinion*, 1922. Free Press Paperbacks by Simon and Schuster.

Maslow, Abraham H. *Motivation and Personality*, 1970. Harper & Row, NY.

Maslow, Abraham H. *Toward a Psychology of Being*, 2011. Wilder Publications.

Mortersen, Kurt W. *Maximum Influence: The 12 Universal Laws of Power Persuasion*, 2004. American Management Association.

Pert, Candace B. *Molecules of Emotion: The Science Behind Mind-Body Medicine*, 2003. Scribner.

Plato. *Symposium*. Translated by Nehamas, Alexander and Paul Woodruff. Hackett Publishing.

Pratkanis, Anthony and Elliot Aronson. *Age of Propaganda: The Everyday Use and Abuse of Persuasion*, 2002. University of California, Holt Paperback.

Reiss, Stephen. *Who am I? The 16 Basic Desires that Motivate Our Actions and Define Our Personalities*, 2000. Berkley Books, NY.

Robbins, Stephen P. *Organizational Behavior*. Pearson Education, Australia.

Ross, Jeffries. *Secrets of Speed Seduction Mastery*, 2010. Ghita Services, Inc.

Scott, David M. *The New Rules of Marketing and PR: How to Use Social Media, Online Video, Mobile Applications, Blogs, News Releases, and Viral Marketing to Reach Buyers Directly*, 2011. John Wiley & Sons.

Scott, David M. *Real Time Marketing*, 2011. John Wiley & Sons.

Streeter, Michael. *Hypnosis: Secrets of the Mind,* 2004. Quarto Publishing.

Tiger, Lionel and Robin Fox. *The Imperial Animal,* 1971. Holt, Rineheart and Wilson.

Trotter, Wilfred. *Instincts of the Herd in Peace and War,* 2007. The Macmillan Company, NY.

Tsu, Sun. *The Art of War.* Translated by Griffith, Samuel B. Oxford University Press.

Yanilov, Eyal and Imi Sde-Or. *Krav Maga: How to Defend Yourself Against Armed Assault,* 2001. Dekel Publishing, Israel.

"The challenge remains. On the other side are formidable forces: money, political power, the major media. On our side are the people of the world and a power greater than money or weapons: the truth. Truth has a power of its own. Art has a power of its own. That age-old lesson— that everything we do matters—is the meaning of the people's struggle here in the United States and everywhere. A poem can inspire a movement. A pamphlet can spark a revolution. Civil disobedience can arouse people and provoke us to think, when we organize with one another, when we get involved, when we stand up and speak out together, we can create a power no government can suppress. We live in a beautiful country. But people who have no respect for human life, freedom, or justice have taken it over. It is now up to all of us to take it back."

(HOWARD ZINN)